SKETCHES OF THE ISLAND OF NEGROS

For Carlos Locsin and Enriqueta Gamboa Locsin of Hacienda Tagbanon who many years ago graciously welcomed an unknown and dusty traveler (directly off the bus from Dumaguete) and whose responsive friendship has been valued since that day in 1951.

* * * * * * * * * * *

Author's Background

Donn V. Hart is Professor of Anthropology and Director of the Center for Southeast Asia Studies at Northern Illinois in DeKalb. He was awarded his Ph.D. degree from Syracuse University and has done post-graduate work at Yale. He was a Fulbright Fellow on several occasions and has written extensively about the Philippines. He is the Editor of the *Philippine Studies Bulletin* and Executive Secretary of the Philippine Studies Committee.

Robustiano Echaúz'

SKETCHES OF THE ISLAND OF NEGROS

Translated and Annotated by

Donn V. Hart

with an

Historical Introduction by

John A. Larkin

Ohio University
Center for International Studies
Papers in International Studies
Southeast Asia Series No. 50
1978

Library of Congress Cataloging in Publication Data

Echaúz, Robustiano.
Sketches of the island of Negros.

(Papers in international studies : Southeast Asia series ; no. 50)
Translation of Apuntes de la isla de Negros.
Bibliography: p.
Includes index.
1. Negros, Philippines. I. Title. II. Series.
DS688.N5E413 959.9'5 78-13403
ISBN 0-89680-070-9

ISBN 0-89680-070-9

TABLE OF CONTENTS

LIST OF ILLUSTRATION

PREFACE

Donn V. Hart

My fascination with Negros and its people was the main reason that led to this translation. Various other reasons also contributed. One was that *Sketches of the Island of Negros* today is available in only a few libraries in the United States--and probably even fewer in the Philippines--although Echaúz' description of late nineteenth century Negros is a valuable account. His book is superior to Francisco Varona's chatty and superficial *Negros: Historia Anecdotica de Su Riqueza y de Sus Hombres* (Manila, 1938).* José E. Marcos' *Reseña Historica de la Isla de Negros Desde los Tiempos Mas Remotos hasta Nuestros Dias* (Manila, 1912) must be firmly rejected as untrustworthy for reasons documented by Scott (1968).

Another reason for this translation involves Echaúz' approach to his subject. Although burdened with the ethnocentric concepts widely shared in the late nineteenth century, he was more than an amateur anthropologist. For instance, he had read and given some heed to one of the most influential anthropological books of his period, Edward Tylor's *Primitive Culture*. His elaborate descriptions of a cockfight, wake, or picnic at a fish corral, although often exasperatingly ornate in style, could only have been written by a perceptive participant observer.

Echaúz writes intimately and warmly about the life of the field hands and sugar mill workers in western Negros. Only one who had attended many all-night wakes in the rural Philippines could describe so knowingly its merry mood. His detailed comments on their food could only be the result of sharing many meals with the barriofolk. His satirical caricatures, whether of a local folk curer or of a minor municipal official, although sometimes gross and mean, are nevertheless convincing and lifelike. Although his knowledge of the *infieles* probably was largely at second hand, he recognized them as humans with both faults and

---

*It was impossible to locate a single copy of Varona's book in the United States. Mr. Carlos Locsin, Victorias, Negros Occidental, has a complete set of 127 installments of both the Spanish text and English translation of Varona's book, as reprinted in the *Country Post*, a defunct bi-weekly newspaper published in Bacolod by Jerry L. Locsin.

virtues. He clearly realized the necessity of eventually incorporating them into the socioeconomic life of Negros. Echaúz' interest in the "little people" of Negros is a unique and valuable attribute of his book.

Another valuable attribute of Echaúz' book is his concern with the development, expansion, and improvement of the sugar industry in Negros whose western province today is known as the "Sugar Bowl of the Philippines." He was active in trying to solve the many problems that then hampered the growing sugar industry of the Island. In fact, he was elected president of an organization established to accomplish this purpose. He wrote several articles dealing with agriculture and local customs for the magazine *El Porvenir de Bisayas*, printed in Iloilo. These articles were signed by him with the pseudonym "*He* [Hacienda] *Manapla*." In 1880, according to Varona, Echaúz headed a provincial list of honor where most of those named were sugar planters (1938:18th Installment). He was an intimate friend of Fathers Cuenca and Mauricio Ferrero, both active in the economic development of Negros.

A final reason for this translation is to encourage the continued study of the history of Negros and its hospitable people. Recently this history has been the subject of two excellent books, Ma. Fe Hernaez Romero's *Negros Occidental Between Two Foreign Powers: 1888-1909* (Manila, 1974) and Angel Martinez Cuesta, O.A.R., *Historia de la Isla de Negros, Filipinas: 1565-1898* (Madrid, 1974). Both books are notable contributions to the history of Negros. Cuesta's book was based on extensive use of archives in Spain and represents only part of his original dissertation (to be published in English translation in the future). Romero's book is a significant contribution "to the growing collection of local studies which have appreciably improved the state of Philippine historiography" (Larkin 1975:174).

My own interest in Negros is of long-standing. Since 1950 I have traveled extensively throughout Negros--by airplane, car, bus, boat, horse, and on foot. I have shared a sleeping mat in many a nipa hut in the still isolated interior of the Island, been regally entertained in *conventos*, comfortably accommodated in the elementary school's Home Economics department's "model room," and enthusiastically honored at the local fiesta--often as an unexpected but welcomed stranger. I have always been treated with unpretended warmth and have enjoyed the bountiful hospitality of the Filipino. This is especially true of the gracious residents of Caticugan, that pleasant village in southern Negros, snugly tucked between Panligiran's bambooed hills and the shallow, noisy Siaton river. This modest effort to encourage the continued study of the history and customs of Negros acknowledges, but in no way repays, the countless favors received from the people of this Island. I hope it is a creditable token of sincere appreciation.

Who was Echaúz?

My research in the United States has uncovered only a few basic facts about the life of Robustiano Echaúz. I am all the more grateful to Father Martinez Cuesta for additional information that he located in Spanish archives.

Echaúz was born in Alfar (Logrono), Spain, but his birth date is unknown. He was Judge of the Court of First Instance in Bacolod from 1881-1885. In March, 1885, the Governor-General of the Philippines issued a writ transferring Echaúz from Bacolod to a less important judgeship in Abra, Luzon. The reason given for the transfer was that Echaúz did not live in the government house in Bacolod with the other provincial officials. His failure to reside with his colleagues was seen as a restriction on his independence of action as a judge. Echaúz was known also to have a financial investment in a Negros hacienda, probably near Manapla; authorities may have regarded this as constituting a conflict of interest.

The notification of his transfer included the statement that "it completes the duties of this Court to inform your Excellency that Judge Robustiano Echaúz is intelligent in the discharge of his duties." (Cf. *Informe de la Sala de Gobierno de la Real Audiencia de Manila*, February 23, 1885, AHN, *Ultramar*, 2331, No. 32). A royal order of November 6, 1885, sent by the overseas ministry to the Governor-General of the Philippines a week later, approved the termination of Echaúz' career as a lawyer (Cf. *Gaceta de Manila*, February 13, 1886). The date of his death is unknown.

Problems of Translation

The English translation of this book (a kind of endeavor Ezra Pound described as a most "desolate undertaking") presented certain problems as do all similar projects. First, there was need to determine the precise meaning of various Spanish terms at that specific time and place. *Almas* and *infieles* have been translated respectively as Christians and non-Christians. In theory, all baptized Filipinos were listed by the Spaniards as in the former category, no matter how physically or administratively remote they were from the Church. Supposedly all *infieles* were non-Christians, although it is possible that some so listed were Christians for one may question the accuracy of Spanish population censuses. However, as Echaúz indicates, the *infieles* had overlaid some Christian concepts upon their animism.

Indocumentados clearly refers to migrant seasonal workers from Panay and Cebu. Since *sacadas* is used today for these Filipino sugar workers, this word has been substituted for *indocumentados*. Vagueness is recognized in the translations of *datu*, *reyezuelo*, and similar terms as leader or chief. For this reason the actual Spanish or Filipino term often is included after its English translation.

The basic source for defining the meaning of Hiligaynon (Panayan) words was the dictionary of Father J. Kaufmann, M.H.M. Father Kaufmann lived in Panay for many years and his dictionary is still the most complete for this language. (Its publication date is unknown but it probably was printed in the 1930s.) Another Panayan-English dictionary, more recent but less comprehensive, was also consulted (Motus 1971). When necessary, the different spellings in Kaufmann's dictionary have been given for terms found in Echaúz' book, e.g., the substitution of *k* for *c*, *b* for *v*, etc. In several instances vernacular terms could be defined only by consulting the Cebuan (Cebuano)-English dictionaries of Wolff (1972) and Hermosisima and Lopez (1966). Unfortunately, a few Panayan or Spanish terms could not be translated, e.g., names of certain foods, local birds, etc.

The map added to this translation attempts to locate every town, barrio, or hacienda mentioned by Echaúz. Whenever these communities once had a different name (sometimes given by Echaúz), this former name is indicated. For a few places, no source or map consulted was of assistance. However, these omissions are few and for unimportant communities. (See Map 1).

Traduttore-traditore is one sin of translators that it is hoped has been avoided--as much as is possible with sin. Every effort was made to retain Echaúz' spirit and his style that varies from a rather pedestrian prose to passages that are involuted and ornate. When he writes about the business of raising sugar, his style is matter-of-fact, the sentences are shorter, and the paragraphs less involved. However, he delights in describing certain events (e.g., a cockfight) or the natural beauties of Negros in an elaborately flowery style. On entering such a paragraph, one has the feeling that once inside, escape from the maze is impossible. In such instances, I partly rewrote the material for clarity's sake.

Acknowledgements

I wish gratefully to acknowledge the skilled assistance received from Peggy Salovesh whose knowledge of idiomatic Spanish, anthropology, and Latin American cultures in general was of great value. Mr. Carlos Locsin, Victorias, Negros Occidental, aided me in the translation of Spanish terms associated with the manufacture of sugar in the Island that dictionaries failed to list. Dr. Mimi Trosdal of Cebu City was also helpful in improving parts of the translation. Dr. Bruce Cruikshank and Dr. Norman Owen, both recognized historians of the Philippines, helped when called upon. I am most grateful to Dr. John A. Larkin for his interest in this project, and his splendid Introduction. Finally, I acknowledge a grant from the Graduate School of Northern Illinois University that greatly speeded the completion of the translation. The Department of Anthropology aided in the preparation of the final manuscript.

INTRODUCTION

NEGROS: AN HISTORICAL PERSPECTIVE

John A. Larkin

Although Robustiano Echaúz chose all of Negros Island as his subject in *Apuntes de la Isla de Negros*, he knew best and wrote most about its western half, the fabled sugar region of the central Philippines. People familiar with the Archipelago associate this region with endless fields of sugar cane and prosperous *hacenderos* who enjoy a life of great luxury. In the contemporary context this means Mercedes cars, spacious mansions, and jet travel, both domestic and foreign. In earlier eras the image of planter life was one of elegant carriages, grand balls, and feudal life on sumptuous estates. While planters have raised great quantities of sugar on Luzon (especially the provinces of Pampanga, Tarlac, Laguna, and Batangas), Panay and Leyte, the growers of Negros, both past and present, seem most suited to the title "Sugar Baron." Wealth and achievement have conferred exalted status upon them, and to the present they have been listed among the most prominent elite in the Philippines. Leading social clubs and charities always have sought to add their family names to membership and sponsorship lists.

Perhaps the Negrenses became the most famous of the planter nobility because their base, the northern portion of Negros Occidental Province, emerged as the most productive region in the country, surpassing its nearest challenger, Pampanga. Another probable reason was that in the twentieth century Negros first converted to modern centrals, those factories which made export sugar a major dollar earner for the colony and later for the country. Or possibly it was because its sugarmen provided political leadership in the highest councils of state. From their ranks came José Luzuriaga to sit as one of the original members of the Philippine Commission. Throughout the American period and the years of the Republic, Negros Occidental supplied leaders in the executive, judicial, and legislative branches. In 1957 José Yulo, a Negrense planter, ran for the nation's highest office, the presidency of the Philippines.

The printed word also has enhanced the Negrenses' national reputation. Planters always have received lavish praise in the local and national press and have found admirers among historians as well. Francisco Varona's 1938 study of Negros reads like a panegyric to the heroic efforts of the Island's nineteenth century agricultural entrepreneurs and their twentieth century heirs. He turned *hacenderos* into superheroes who alone created the province's economic success. Varona's enthusiasm far surpassed that of Echaúz' *Apuntes* from which he drew much of his material.

Echaúz possessed the advantage of witnessing the unfolding of northern Negros into a vast agricultural plain; indeed, he participated in that drama. He viewed the planting families as they ascended from their condition as early tentative settlers to established landed gentry. Echaúz knew, or heard about directly, those individuals, priests, officials, and merchants who encouraged and buttressed the efforts of the first *hacenderos*. He comprehended more of the totality of effort necessary to convert a wilderness into a highly productive expanse of plantations. We are fortunate to have this realistic observation of Negros' first important historical phase, the latter half of the nineteenth century.

The enormous increase in sugar production, stimulated by the opening of the neighboring port of Iloilo to world commerce, made the years 1855 to 1898 remarkable ones for Negros. In that era the Island's exports multiplied from 190 metric tons in 1850 to 113,850 in 1893. Technological improvement could be measured by the 274 steam sugar mills operating in 1893, whereas none existed when the era began. The agricultural revolution so changed Negros that its western population increased from 36,000 (1850) to 308,000 (1903); the number of municipalities expanded from six to thirty-four. In 1890 the Spanish administration recognized the population rise by splitting the territory into two provinces, Negros Occidental and Negros Oriental. It was this transition to which Echaúz bore witness.

It may be helpful while reading *Apuntes* to know something of the time which preceded this great era of change as events before 1850 tend to highlight what followed. At this period Negros could best be characterized as a wilderness largely ignored by the Spaniards. Even before they came in the late sixteenth century, the Island (then called Buglas) suffered from neglect. The meager available evidence of pre-Hispanic times reveals only that there were few inhabitants who lived some distance inland from the coast. The early Negrenses practiced farming chiefly because the flourishing Chinese trade along the western coast of the Archipelago largely bypassed Buglas. Bands of Filipino Muslims (Moros) raided its beaches and villages in search of slaves, offering an additional incentive for the natives to live inland.

Who were these natives? Nearest to the shoreline dwelled a population of Filipinos of Malayan heritage who raised wet rice in paddies and dry rice in their mountain swiddens (shifting agriculture). Others kept to the dense forest tracks where they hunted the abundant game which originally roamed the Island. These Bisayan Filipinos may have been outnumbered by Negritos, migratory hunters, and food gatherers who collected such exotic forest products as tough vines (rattan, etc.) for cordage, beeswax, and substances useful in folk medicines. These products they sold to whatever foreign traders might occasionally come to the Island. The Negritos, now largely restricted to the most remote interior of the Island, must have been numerous and visible in the sixteenth century for the early Spanish visitors started calling the Island Negros.

In 1565 the Adelantado (King's representative) Miguel de Legaspi sent to Negros the first Spanish expedition under the leadership of the pilot Esteban Rodriguez. His crew and he circumnavigated the Island touching land at several points, especially along the western coast. These first contacts were met by strong Negrense hostility; Rodriguez' Indonesian interpreter died from a spear wound sustained in one encounter. The immediate unfriendly response of the local inhabitants, undoubtedly based on their harrowing experience with Moro raiders, suggests that they feared and distrusted all strangers. Because of the inhospitality of the populace and the mountainous terrain, the lack of a deep-water port,* as well as their own special interest in Luzon, the Spaniards did little to settle or develop Negros for the next six years.

Only in 1571 did Legaspi assign to some of his followers *encomiendas*, those tax farms of early years, on Negros. The *encomenderos*, however, preferred not to move to such a wilderness to collect taxes and supervise native conversion to Roman Catholicism. Far more attractive opportunities obtained elsewhere in Cebu and Luzon where populous and wealthy *encomiendas* were not too far from Spanish settlements. To the Spaniards Negros remained an unattractive and isolated station to be administered by officials assigned there by Manila. The *Indios* (Filipinos) of the central Philippines considered the Island a remote almost uninhabited place where a goddess named Lalahon resided in Canlaon volcano.

From the outset Negros was a disappointment to the Spaniards for initial information that the Island contained gold proved false. The Island's wealth mainly consisted of a common variety of agricultural and forest products such as rice,

---

*Either the Spaniards at this time did not know of Bonbonon (see Echaúz, p. 1) or they did not consider it useful. Its remote location in southern Negros has always negated any possible advantages this barrio had as a port facility.

coconuts, beeswax, a material called *medriñaque*, *cabo negro*, an extremely durable palm whose fiber was made into ship's cable, and palm wine. (*Medriñaque* is fabric made from abaca or palm fiber and is used as a lining for women's dresses.) With these products the Negrenses met their annual tribute obligations paid to the few government servants who came to oversee its accumulation. Since the Spanish government never could find sufficient officials to supervise affairs, they limited their residences to a few key settlements along the coast, mainly at Tanjay, Ilog, and Binalbagan. From these places the tribute went to Cebu or Arevalo (near modern Iloilo), the latter a large and prosperous town on adjacent Panay.

By the beginning of the seventeenth century the position of Negros within the Spanish empire had solidified and remained almost static for the next 250 years. A *corregidor* (military governor) stationed at Ilog represented colonial authority, although tax payments in kind continued to be sent to Panay and Cebu from the western and eastern shores respectively until 1734. In this year the Spaniards transformed Negros into a single administrative and revenue collection district with its capital (*cabecera*) at Ilog. However, most produce taken as tribute, especially rice, went to feed the colony and garrison on grain-poor Cebu.

Corregidores seem to have done little to promote better conditions and as late as the 1840s no adequate roads or permanent government buildings existed. These officials had some excuse for their inactivity in public works because the Island faced, without much help from Manila, frequent devastation by Moros who ravaged the coasts especially in the eighteenth, but also the nineteenth, century. Although each *corregidor*, after 1734, had a military attaché to assist him with defense, the protection of the shoreline remained inadequate. At least some *corregidores* faced this external threat by removing to Iloilo, leaving the general population when raids occurred the choice of fleeing temporarily inland or living permanently in the interior to escape danger. The government left the Negrenses without any real means of improving their welfare and with imperfect guarantees for their personal safety.

The little support Spain provided to Negros came chiefly from the Church. From their few parishes in the coastal lowlands, a small group of priests, sometimes members of the friar orders, at others Spanish or native Filipino seculars, administered sacraments, served as missionaries to the wandering peoples, and offered solace after Moro raids. Given the dearth of priests available, especially for so isolated a place as Negros, the pastoral effort began slowly. Augustinians arrived first to establish their initial missions at Binalbagan (1575), Tanjay (1580), and Ilog (1584). However, they lacked manpower to maintain their commitment and by 1587 had abandoned these missions, causing Bishop Salazar to lament that the natives were reverting to idolatry. The Augustinians preferred to concentrate on crucial parishes in wealthier, more populous places in the Philippines.

Only after 1600 in Tanjay and 1630 in Ilog did these communities gain pastoral attention, when Jesuits received assignments to visit them as part of their general Bisayan responsibility. Scattered Spanish seculars and, from 1622 to 1638, one or two Recollects, labored mainly at Binalbagan. The Jesuits gradually extended their sway over the southern portion of Negros, as far down the coast as Sipalay and Dumaguete and into the interior to Kabankalan and several mission stations. By the eighteenth century the Jesuits were joined in their efforts by secular priests and together they managed as many as six parishes on the west coast but only two on the eastern side.

When the Crown exiled the Jesuits from the Philippines in 1768, their Negros congregations were taken over by the Dominicans who, faced with many obligations elsewhere, shortly handed over these newly acquired stations to Filipino secular priests. From the 1770s until the mid-nineteenth century, native Fathers had charge of large parishes including many *visitas* which stretched from Cauayan as far north as Silay on the west coast and Siaton to Tanjay on the east. The vast expanse of these parishes necessarily meant that ministerial care was thinly extended. Echaúz notes that as late as the 1850s many Bisayan superstitions prevailed even in the lowlands. Religious care in Negros, although more consistent and substantial than government services, proved deficient because of inadequate commitment on the part of the Church.

The state of Negros' economy scarcely showed any real advancement before the 1850s. A lack of permanent church buildings indicated not only insufficient attention to evangelization but also poor economic conditions. Since the coming of Spain little change had occurred in agriculture. A government report of 1739 revealed that the Island still met its tax obligations largely with the same produce it shipped in the sixteenth and seventeenth centuries, i.e., rice, *cabo negro*, and a variety of forest products. This report also listed two new crops, abaca and cacao, as exported from the Island, but the amounts remained insignificant in its overall economy.

Cacao cultivation began through the efforts of a Jesuit, Fray Juan Davila, assigned to the parish of Ilog in the late seventeenth and early eighteenth centuries. Although he brougt cacao to Negros, it never florished as it did on Mindanao. When the Frenchman Jean Mallat wrote about Negros in the late 1830s, he indicated that only small crops of cacao, along with coffee and tobacco, were planted by natives in elevated areas beyond the lowlands (Mallat 1846 I:319-20). On the plains, farmers still harvested mainly rice and some tobacco, *cabo negro*, and abaca.

In the century prior to 1845 external trade was dominated by the governor (*alcalde mayor*) by his right of the *indulto de comercio*, a privilege and inducement granted to augment otherwise meager salaries. In exchange for fabric imported from Manila, Negros *alcaldes* shipped rice surpluses and small amounts of tobacco to the capital. Chinese mestizos handled remaining rice, forest produce, fish, and pearls which went to their home port of Cebu. The only other commercial activity on Negros invovled some cottage industry weaving of such native fabrics as *lompotes* (cotton cloth) and *sinamay* (abaca cloth), commissioned by the great mestizo cloth merchants of Molo and Jaro, Panay. Undoubtedly, once Iloilo began shipping to international ports, the commercial contacts with Negros provided the Panay merchants with knowledge about its agricultural possibilities.

Perhaps a few general observations will help to put Echaúz' account of nineteenth century Negros in a clearer perspective. What he described was the taming of a vast frontier, a phenomenon in many parts of the world at this time. With the quickening of economic growth stimulated by the industrial revolution, pioneers were moving to virgin land in North and South America, Africa, Australia, and Asia. This expansion exhibited a number of common characteristics no matter where it occurred or who participated. Land previously lightly populated, and frequently covered with impressive stands of timber, was converted by the ax and plow into farms mainly devoted to commercial crops but, in some cases, to food crops for the burgeoning world population which increasingly found employment in nonagricultural pursuits.

Negros fitted this pattern since its growth resulted from North America's expanding sugar consumption. As the nineteenth century progressed the United States took an ever larger share of Philippine sugar until the McKinley tariff severely limited that market in the 1890s. In this decade Europe and Asia started to absorb some of the surplus sugar. Conditions in the sugar industry showed steady improvement until the time of the Philippine Revolution when the combination of war and failing economic conditions caused a temporary reversal. By this time much of northern Negros Occidental had been settled and a significant portion of its timber removed.

The destruction of great stands of Philippine hardwoods represents a second aspect of the taming of the wilderness which Negros shared with other contemporary frontier settlements of the world. In every case the ecological biosphere (the original natural habitat) was severely altered at great expense to the flora and fauna. Sometimes the natural resources went into world markets for the profit of exploiters. In other cases, such as Negros, the valuable forests vanished to make way for farming.

Not until the twentieth century, when world supplies had notably diminished, did lumberers start to sell timber from interior northern Negros. Aside from the obvious loss of animals and vegetation, the full extent of the ecological damage caused by this great movement onto the frontier will never be known for visitors and local commentators left no remarks about soil management. Not surprisingly in a time when land came so cheap and seemed so limitless, few people, if any, considered preserving it as a birthright for future generations.

A third characteristic associated with the conquest of almost all great world frontiers was the elimination, through absorption or extermination, of the original, frequently aboriginal, peoples of these territories. Through generations of adaptation, these inhabitants had come to be part of the ecological balance, dependent upon it as well as shaping it. When that system fell before the onslaught of aggressive forces, its human component also diminished. Echaúz dramatically demonstrated this pattern for Negros in Chapter XII with the story of the death of Manyabog and his followers at Carolan. This bloody event, perhaps exaggerated in the telling--perhaps not--may have represented an extreme way of coping with these early residents of the Island. However, it does reveal the inevitable clash between the primitive and civilized worlds, almost always resulting in the disappearance of the former.

When the Spaniards first arrived in Negros they found two types of forest dwellers, the Negritos and wandering groups of Malayan ancestry, part farmers and part hunters and gatherers, who occasionally interacted with their lowland rice growing neighbors for trading purposes. The latter group, variously known as Bukidnons, Montes, Mangyans, Mondos, Carolanos, and Ambaks, have survived, and continue to do so, by retreating before the modern farmers and lumberers with their more powerful technology. But as Echaúz astutely noticed, in latter nineteenth century many of them assimilated into the lowland population through the missionary endeavors of the Recollect friars who converted them to Catholicism and settled them in permanent communities. Such efforts by the priests aided the sugar boom, for many of the new Christians joined the ever deficient labor force needed to clear new land and work the plantations. Conversion of the pagan peoples not only disorganized their indigenous culture but also contributed to the spread of sugar cultivation across the Negros wilderness.

Finally, every world frontier enormously enriched a select few individuals who, more than all other pioneers, reaped the treasures the wilderness yielded. From place to place and time to time the commodities differed, e.g., pelts, timber, minerals, cash crops, or strategically located property; however, in each area certain persons, by dint of special skill, extraordinary effort, shrewd investments, or a combination of these factors, monopolized the rewards. They found ways to secure concessions, control a labor force, and apply mechanical techniques to the purpose of exploiting natural resources on a huge scale, far grander than any single settler could achieve through his own means.

This circumstance of great wealth accruing through the labors of many and the power of machines has created something of a discrepancy between an important segment of frontier mythology and the reality of its conquest. The greatest exploiters, those most admired in song and tale for their achievements and wealth, the rugged individualists *par excellence*, the most vaunted heroes of the wilderness, owed most to corporate effort. Their schemes may have separated them from the rest in the opinion of others, but the execution of those plans called for the contributions of many.

This paradox applies as accurately to Negros as to any other frontier. Its original pioneer planters, those progenitors of the modern sugar aristocracy, depended upon the efforts of numerous field hands to raze the forest and thicket and to put the first sugar points into the cleared earth. None of them created alone great estates with their own hands. In fact, they began in several different fashions, each one demanding use of a considerable labor force. The earliest of the new settlers to Negros, who arrived in the 1840s, brought with them workers whom they led from old settlements to found new towns and plantations. People like the Spaniard Don Agustin Montilla and his wife Dona Vicenta Locsin reshaped Pulupandan from a sitio of Bago into a flourishing agricultural community and municipality. Montilla invested his own effort and capital in this project and had a fort built at his own expense to protect his followers from the Moros. He underwent the ordeal of captivity at their hands and had to be ransomed from their homeland of Sulu. This extremely romantic figure established an enormous personal estate; however, it should be noted that he brought with him to Pulupandan a group of 118 farm laborers and their families to do the manual work.

From the 1850s on other founding families came from Cebu, Bohol, and especially from Panay. Some brought their field hands with them, some hired transient workers from other islands, and some acquired help from among the Negrenses, including the newly-converted hill peoples. Both the Recollects and Spanish government troops deserve recognition for their role in making possible the new plantations.

Parenthetically, the Recollects and the military gave other kinds of assistance as well. One of the clergy, Father Fernando Cuenca of Talisay, constructed the first functional water wheel on the Island and was instrumental in starting the first major road building project. The Spanish Navy using steam vessels, finally ended the Moro raids, encouraging more rapid migration of people to Negros.

A final method of entering the sugar business involved the direct purchase of already functioning plantations. A number of the original Chinese mestizo entrepreneurs from Iloilo, who had backgrounds in the cloth business, saw sugar as a good speculation. They made direct purchases of haciendas with their fields, machines, draught animals, buildings, and labor force. Bisayan newspapers in the late nineteenth and early twentieth century carried advertisements offering such Negros estates for sale.

One can view the founding fathers of the Negros' sugar industry as energetic and clear-sighted entrepreneurs who received enormous amounts of help in creating their fortunes. In the twentieth century their descendants built upon their early efforts and continued the province's leadership in sugar production. After a decade of depression sugar boomed again as the American market reopened following the passage of the Payne-Aldrich Tariff Act in 1909. The introduction of sugar centrals in 1913 inaugurated a second technological revolution. The new wealth which came about in the wake of these innovations merely served to amplify the reputation of the sugarmen. Their opulence and government service enhanced their stature at the expense of others who contributed equally to the growth of the sugar business.

Within modern Philippine society no individual possesses more prestige than the sugar *hacendero*. While there are other roads to prominence, politics and the professions for example, a large number of successful people demonstrate their personal achievement by buying agricultural property, frequently sugar land. Not long ago a planter in Bacolod spoke to me of his wonderment at the multitude of Filipinos from outside Negros, especially Manila, who desired to acquire even a relatively small plot of sugar land. Since most of these newcomers did not wish to come to farm the soil, he guessed they wished only to own the property so they could call themselves *hacenderos*! My informant lamented this sad state of affairs because he felt that those who managed the land themselves, especially the old planters, garnered fuller yields and took greater care of the land for future generations.

* * * * * * * * * * *

The publication of this translation of *Apuntes* comes at a time of great change in Philippine historiography. For more than a decade historians have been shifting their focus to new subjects and ingeniously adapting the methodology of other academic disciplines to the solution of historical problems. Whereas before they concentrated on Manila-centric affairs of national consideration, and the lives of great Filipinos, they have now increasingly turned to an examination of provincial and village life and changes in rural society.

Inevitably, this shift of interest has led away from the traditional political and administrative history associated with insular-wide affairs, to a social history which borrows heavily from such disciplines as anthropology, sociology, and agricultural economics. Theory from these fields has been applied to the different types of data available for local studies because the evidence, often scanty and disparate, requires innovative analysis. Moreover, the main concerns of rural inhabitants, agriculture, poverty, and folk culture are better illuminated by the new historical approach. Many fine examples of this new social history, now existing in the form of university theses, will gradually become available in published form over the next several years. In time they will serve as a basis for a major reinterpretation of Philippine history which will reveal the crucial role of rural affairs on the nation and de-emphasize the foreigner as the major mover in Filipino affairs.

This reinterpretation, so clearly needed, cannot come too soon. What historians require most is new, more revealing data on rural change, the kind of detail which Echaúz abundantly provides in his perceptive glimpse of Negros. We are fortunate to have his work made available once more after so many years of neglect. Hopefully, other such studies will appear to assist Philippine historians in their important task.

R[obustiano] Echaúz

APUNTES DE LA ISLA DE NEGROS

MANILA

Tipo-Litografía de Chofré y Companía
Escolta, Number 33
1894

His Excellency, Don Ramón Blanco y Erenas, Marquis of Peña-Plata, Governor-General of the Philippine Islands[1]

On accepting the offering of the dedication of these *Apuntes* to your Excellency, you honored this book and conferred on the Island of Negros a signal favor which she will know how to recompense by giving your title, won in glorious battle, to the most beautiful and the best of all the Missions. This is a remembrance to the illustrious and prudent governor who knew how to bestow protection to those who live by the plow and hard work, and to those who were concerned with the prosperity of such a prized Island.

Who kisses the hand of Your Excellency

R. Echaúz

Manila, March 16th, 1894

---

[1]Ramón Blanco y Erenas was Governor-General of the Philippines from 1893 to 1896.

General Government of the Philippines
Office of the Governor
Section 2
Personnel Department

Having considered the application made by Don R. Echaúz y Pintado[2] to publish a book titled *Apuntes de la Isla de Negros*, this General Government grants the request. Manila. March 15th, 1894 Bolibar.

We, Don Fray Leandro Arrué, of the Discalced Order of San Agustin, by the grace of God and the Holy Apostolic See, Bishop of Jaro [Panay], etc.

By these presents, and insofar as it concerns Us, we grant our license to print and publish the book titled *Apuntes de la Isla de Negros* written by Don R. Echaúz. By virtue of an order given by Our Very Illustrious *Provisor* [ecclesiastical vicar-general] and Administrator *in seda plena*, the book has been examined and contains, according to the censor, no phrase, concept or chapter that should be prohibited. On the contrary, we are of the opinion that the reading of his book is worthy of recommendation to those who desire to know the continuous progress and succinct history of the island of Negros. Episcopal Palace of Jaro, March 27, 1894. Fray Leandro, Bishop. Before me, Fray Eleuterio Aranda, Secretary. Bishopric of Jaro. Registered. Book 7, title 1, folio 371.

---

[2] *Pintado* (Sp. painted) was also the name the early Spaniards gave Bisayans since many of them tattooed their bodies.

TABLE OF CONTENTS[3]

[3]This TABLE OF CONTENTS, called the *Index*, is at the end of Echaúz' book.

---

[4]Although *pacol* (Pan. *pakol*) is "A kind of banana containing many seeds, even more than the *lisohan* [banana]" (Kaufmann n.d.:65), cloth woven from abaca fibers has the same name.

CHAPTER I

GEOGRAPHY OF THE ISLAND OF NEGROS

The island of Negros deserves to be ranked by rights and without argument among the most important islands forming the Philippine archipelago. This is because of its location, surrounding seas, neighboring islands, influencing winds, and lands that form and mountains that dominate the Island. Its valleys, foothills, rivers, and inhabitants, together with their products, work, manufactures, machinery, human efforts and intelligence also contribute to its importance.

Negros, located in the Bisayas, is surrounded by three important nearby islands. It sends to Panay, on the west, its richest products, the result of hard and difficult labor. Negros also maintains commercial relations with Cebu on the east. It remains distant from Mindanao on the south that caused Negros so much distress some years ago when its inhabitants [Muslim Filipinos or Moros] sacked and devastated Negros' best towns, taking captive many people.

Negros is separated from these three islands by straits and seas. Its coast is steep at Pulopandan [Pulupandan]. Bombonon [Bonbonon, Siaton municipality, southern Negros Oriental Province] is a sheltered and easily accessible deep-water port. The shore along Bacolod, Minuluan [Talisay] and Silay is long and flat. At its greatest extension, the island measures north to south 240 kilometers and from east to west, forty to fifty kilometers, totaling 9,000 square kilometers. It is 300 miles from Manila. From Iloilo, crossroads of agriculture and commerce for Negros, it is twenty-nine miles to the west coast [of Panay] and seventy to eighty miles to the east (See Map 1).[5]

During the northeast monsoon, the winds from Silanga blow like the winds from Mindanao, Guimaras, and Panay, during the southwest monsoon, over beaches and mangrove swamps, across former forests now cultivated areas and purified by the sea breezes. Cleared lands and the industry of the people have created ideal conditions for cleanliness and for good health on the Island. The rivers along whose banks grow wild sarsaparilla, the potable

---

[5]Alicante (1951) has a large folded map that locates many of the rivers and mountains mentioned by Echaúz.

MAP 1 COMMUNITIES MENTIONED IN *SKETCHES OF THE ISLAND OF NEGROS*

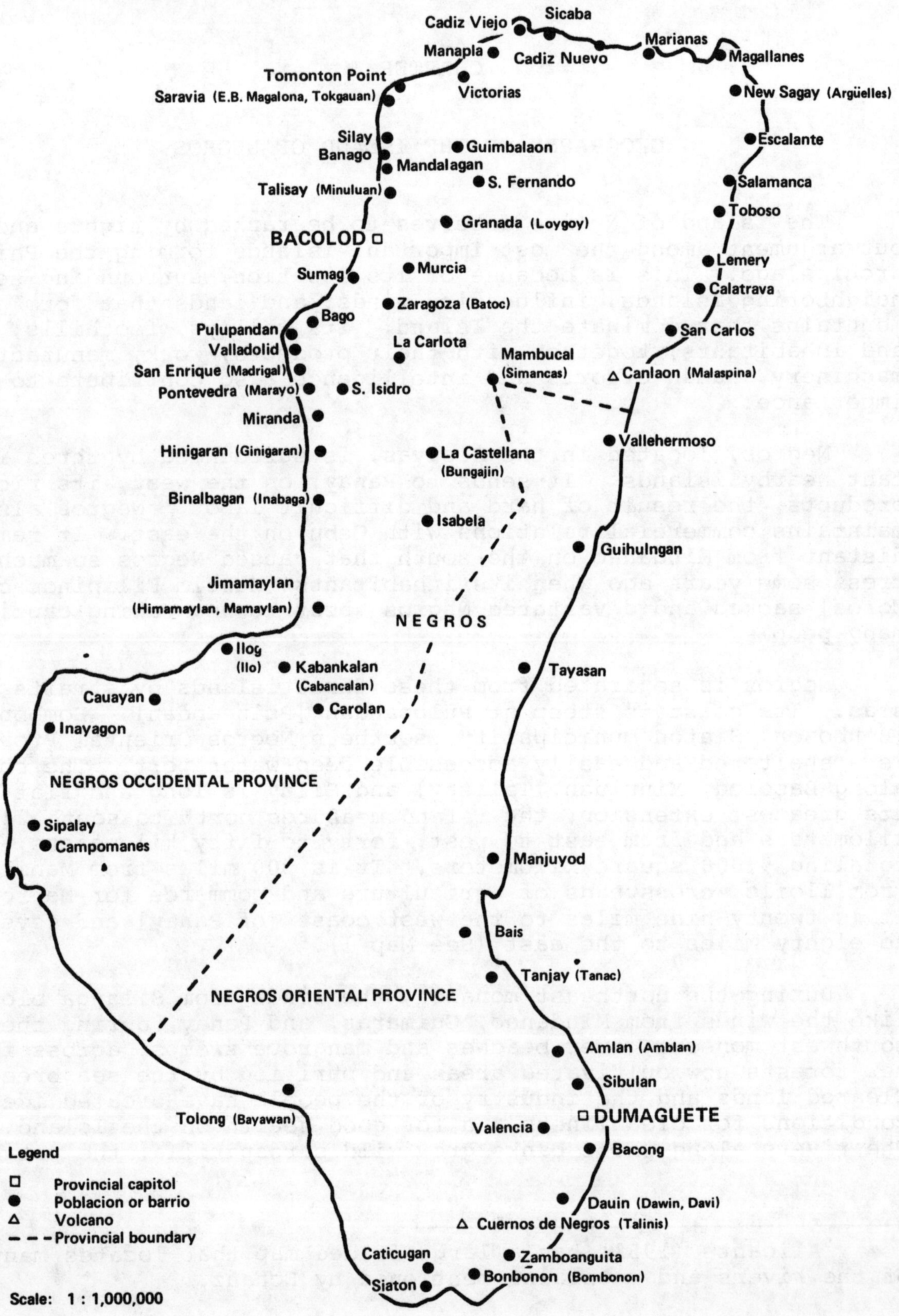

springs, the mountains where grow the *ilang-ilang*[6] quinine, pitch tree (*brea*)[7] and *tagulauay*,[8] a most effective cicatrisant, all favor life by lessening and making up for losses and wear caused by daily work. There are no known endemic illnesses.

The foothills of Marapara and Malaespina [Malaspina or Canlaon], the highest mountains on the Island, are the homes of thousands of industrious people. These mountains send down abundant water for use in navigation and in powering the machines of the sugar industry. They also offer fertile lands where abaca, coffee, and cacao grow, and provide excellent building lumber to the north and south of the Island.

The land of Negros is flat and extended in the western region, where the mountains are more than thirty kilometers away from the coast. In the eastern region, the mountains are nearer the sea except for Dumaguete, Bacon [Bacong], Dauin, and Sibulan, which are some seven kilometers from the foothills. One region as much as the other has within its mountains magnificent valleys and beautiful gorges. Scattered here and there are extensive plains which, because of the quality of the soil, can grow all types of crops.

The mountains of Negros, as named by their inhabitants, are Marapara, Malaespina, Macauili, Mababui, Calactcat del Tinongan, Manacop, Payao de la Isabela, Malibaslibas, Ayuñgon, Carolan, and Tipasi. There is the range from Kabankalan to Bais, Tanjay, Nueva Valencia, Bacon, Zamboanguita, Siaton, Tolón [Tolong], and Sipalay and another range which extends above all these towns on the eastern coast.

The more important rivers which run from the mountains to the sea are Danao, Gimogoan or Marianas, Gitalon, Talaban, Sicaba,

---

[6]*Ilang-ilang* (*Canango odorata* (Lam.) Hooker f. and Thomas) is a plant with fragrant flowers that today is grown commercially (Brown 1957 1:551).

[7]*Brea* (*Canarium aspersum* Bentham) is a large tree (Reyes 1938:162-63). It is also known in Negros Occidental as *salem* and in Cebu as *salong*. A more common name for this tree is *pagsahingin*. However, *Canarium luzonicum* (Blume) A. Gray, commonly known as *pili*, may be the tree referred to by Echaúz since it is "known locally by the Spanish term '*brea blanca* (white pitch)'" (Brown 1954 2:244-47).

[8]*Tagulauay* or *tagulauai* (Panayan) may be the woody vine (*Parameria barbata*) (Blume) K. Schum). The bark is used to make rope and to tie rice bundles. Its rubber-like sap is a snakebite medicine (Brown 1957 3:245).

Chamberí, Manapla, Malijao, Carruguiat, Malógo, Malisbog, Madalag, Imbang, Nahalinan, Silay, Catabla, Matabang, Mandalagan, Lupit, Magsungay, Sumag, Calomangan, Bago, Valladolid, Tinabagan, Pontevedra, Ginigaran, Tanolo, Binalbagan, Aguisan, Tablaban Grande and Pequeño de Jimamaylan, Suay, Tuyuman, Binicuil, Ilog, and Tablas. These rivers flow on the western coast, and during high tide allow entrance to all kinds of vessels with draughts of six or seven feet to reach as far up the rivers as the towns located near their headwaters. The first river, Danao, has sufficient depth for large vessels with deep draughts.[9] This series of rivers originates in the north of the western region and extends to the southern end of the region.

On the eastern coast, the rivers look more like torrents, rushing to the sea, not permitting even smaller vessels to enter with the exception of Tanjay where high tide permits the *lorchas* and larger boats from Iloilo to be loaded.

THE SOILS AND SUBSOILS of the island of Negros are of three kinds, named in Bisayan, *Salamayon*,[10] *Banicá*,[11] and *Abô-abô*.[12] The first one is composed of humus, clay, and sand in such proportions as to make a thick layer of one to three meters of humus. It is excellent for sugar cane, abaca, coffee, cacao, tobacco, indigo, rice, mongo beans, corn, and all kinds of root crops. Its subsoil is calcareous.

---

[9]Most of the rivers of Negros, with a few exceptions, could not be used extensively for shipping sugar from the interior to the sea. Many of the rivers were too shallow, while others had sandbars at their mouths. The Danao river in the mountainous extreme northeast of Negros was one exception but little sugar was produced in this region. Flat-bottomed *lorchas* could penetrate from five to ten kilometers from the sea on the Bago, Binalbagan, and Ilog rivers. The *lorcha* (Pan. *cortsa*) is a wide, flat-bottomed cargo boat of about fifty tons pulled by a sailboat or tug. When necessary, the *lorcha* could be poled in shallow rivers. (See also Kaufmann n.d.:513.) "It is owing to this lack of large rivers and harbors suitable for seagoing craft that no sugar is exported [1908-1909] directly from Negros, but all is taken across in small sailing boats to Iloilo, the nearest port" (Walker 1910:11).

[10]*Salamayon* means "Streaked, interspersed with" (Kaufmann n.d.:807).

[11]*Banicá* is a type of clay soil. A common expression in Negros Occidental is "As hard as *Banicá*."

[12]*Abô* ("ash") also means "Ash coloured, ashy pale, gray" (Kaufmann n.d.:5). The best source for the soils of Negros Occidental is Alicante (1951) but he does not use any of the local names for soils mentioned by Echaúz.

The second kind of soil, *Banicá*, formed from sand and humus, well mixed, is a first class soil. It is suited for all types of seeds and plants, bamboo, and lumber. The subsoil is cretaceous in some parts and stony in others. Soil of this kind contains one to three meters of humus.

The third type of soil, *Abó-abó*, is composed of a small layer of humus and a large quantity of sand which forms a humus layer of two to three feet. It produces well in a rainy year but in dry times plants do not grow well because the sun penetrates almost to their roots. The subsoil is stony with a mixture of marl. *Abó-abó* soil is the least desired by the farmer. It is good that this kind of soil is found in only a few pockets in certain zones of the Island.

DIALECTS: *Panayano Hiligaino* [*Hiligaynon*] is spoken in the western [Occidental] and Cebuan in the eastern [Oriental] region. Both languages are derived from Bisaya. They differ in some words, and Cebuan has more contractions than the first. The structure of articles, nouns, pronouns, verbs, and conjugations are similar, as belonging to the same language family.

MEDICINAL WATERS: These waters abound and do much good for the persons who go where they are found. Outstanding among these are the waters of Mambucal in Murcia, on the slopes of Canlaon, where six springs of different kinds of water have a rapid efficacy on one who enjoys them. Ferruginous and hot sulfur springs also exist in Minuluan, Granada, Jimamaylan [Hímamaylan], Isabela, Guadalupe, Guimbalaon, and Dauin.

The population of Negros consists of *Peninsulars* [Spaniards born in Spain but residing in the Philippines] who are dedicated to agriculture. *Naturales* [Filipinos] live in the towns (*pueblos*) and haciendas and work in the fields. The *Insulares*[13] [Spaniards born in the Philippines] live in the greatest liberty, unsubjugated, and either clear the forests or do nothing. Unbaptized and unsubdued *infieles* [non-Christians] have an aptitude for work. And there are the Negritos or Aetas, spiritless, indolent, rachitic, weak, and without any regard for work.

---

[13]In this context, Echaúz appears to use *Insulares* to mean Christian Filipinos who live in remote areas beyond the reach of the government and the Church. Elsewhere in his book, Echaúz uses *Natural* to mean "native." Therefore, at times, depending upon its context, *Natural* could mean Christian or non-Christian. Locsin's translation of Varona gives "pagan" as the English term for *Natural* (1965: 22nd installment). By Echaúz' time the former name for Filipinos, *Indios*, had become a pejorative term, and hence is not used by the author (Cushner 1971:266).

The first two groups, the Spaniards and Filipinos (*Naturales*), follow customs suited to a perfect civilization and are of the Catholic faith. The others, living independently outside any government or jurisdiction, will be the object of this brief study that will probe into the causes and motives behind certain mutinies and rebellions that surprise non-residents of the Island. The military authorities are forced to initiate campaigns, which result only in momentary pacification, for these people soon return to rebellion. It is almost certain that this state of unrest will cease with the establishment of the planned missionary parishes and settlements. These missions are the only instruments capable of this work of redemption. Their final objective is the subjugation of thousands and thousands of individuals removed from society for causes inherent in their temperament and conditions ingrained in their tastes and predilections. The missions will be able to complete this work because of the vigor of their ideas and their protection by the authorities.

The Spaniards belong to the white or Caucasian race. The Filipinos (*Naturales*) belong to the Malayan race or to the union of Malay and Mongol. The non-Christians are of Malayan origin, differentiated from Filipinos only in customs and practices. The Negritos belong to the race of the same name, and are completely separated from the others by their way of life, lack of the habit of work, and adherence to the territory they inhabit. While the non-Christian Filipinos build houses and live in them, the Negritos wander freely without fixed dwellings, in a certain area of the forest that they regard as their own. There they practice superstitions and enforce their authority over their domain, preventing the Filipinos (*Naturales*) from cutting wood without their permission.

Guided by their instincts the Negritos move through the forest, taking their direction from some animals that look for flowers of shrubs and the fruit of trees. They sleep where night catches them, near embers of fires that give warmth and protection from bothersome insects. They hang their dead in trees, wrapped in mats or fronds of the *palma brava*.[14] Those who die of smallpox or cholera, horrible sicknesses to them, are thrown into the river.

The island of Negros has hardly any history that would result in written accounts or discussions. This lack of data, monuments, objects, and findings is such that the student cannot even guess at, let alone harvest, anything of significance concerning ancient civilizations and moral and intellectual cultures prior to 1521.

---

[14]*Palma brava* (Pan. *anahau* is a palm (*Livistona rotundifolia* (Lam.) Mart.) whose trunks often are used as house posts, spear shafts, and canes and leaves for thatching (Brown 1957 1:312-13).

Figure 1: The Bago river with *lorchas* in the background. (Walker)

Figure 2: Loading sugar on *lorchas* in Negros Occidental. (Walker)

It is known that in 1575 and 1584 the priests' residences[15] of Binalbagan[16] and Ilog were founded. In about 1599, an invasion of Mindanao Moros occurred that razed and burned all the towns on the Island.

In 1622, Fray Francisco de San Nicolás, a native of Cádiz, Spain, made a trip from Negros to Manila. Amazing miracles were told that gave the Recollect Fathers great fame and prestige among the people of Negros.[17] In the same year of 1622, Father Ricardo Fulgencio founded the parish priest's residence of Binalbagan which administered 1,500 families. In 1628, Señor Arce entrusted to said Fathers the district of Bago and other towns on the coast.

In 1628, the Prior of Binalbagan was appointed at the provincial chapters. An exchange was made with the Jesuit Fathers who were given jurisdiction over the towns[18] of Ilog, Kabankalan, Jimamaylan, Cauayan and the missions of Inayauan and Sipalay. All of these towns and missions later came under the control of the secular priests until 1848. In this year His Excellency, the Bishop of Cebu, Don Fray Romualdo Gimeno,[19] informed the Superior Government of Manila of the need to give to the Recollect priests the administration of Negros since secular priests were so scarce. In 1848 the Very Reverend Provincial Fray Joaquin Soriano took possession [of Negros] in the name of the Recollect order.

The dates of the attacks on Negros by the Moros are detailed in the *Breve Reseña de la Diócesis de Cebú*,[20] published by the

---

[15]The priest's residence in the Philippines is called *convento*.

[16]Binalbagan's name is said to be derived from *inabagan*, "a place of refuge" from the *habagat* or southwest monsoon (Saonoy 1972:1).

[17]The Augustine Recollects, a reform branch of the Augustin order, were the last order to come to the Philippines in 1606. During the Spanish period 1,632 Recollect priests came to the Philippines and are credited with founding 235 towns. When the Recollects arrived in the 17th century, they were assigned, in addition to Negros, parishes in Luzon, Mindoro, Masbate, Palawan, and Mindanao. The Jesuits came in 1581, were expelled in 1768, and returned to the Archipelago in 1858 (Gowing 1967:31-35).

[18]*Pueblo* has been translated as town, although on a few occasions, based on the context, municipality was chosen.

[19]Bishop Gimeno's decree, returning the Recollects to Negros, was dated June 20, 1848 (Romero 1974:20).

[20]Felipe Redondo y Sendino. *Breve Reseña de lo que fue y de lo que es la Diócesis de Cebú en las Islas Filipinas* (Manila, 1886).

priest Don Felipe Redondo and in the *Historia General de Filipinas*[21] by Father Fray Juan de la Concepcion, a Recollect Discalced Agustinian, that was published in the town of Sampaloc in 1792. These volumes also give details of the administration of the towns, the proposals made to the *corregidor*[22] by the officers and heads (*cabezas*) of the three divisions of Negros, reports by Fray Matias Guerrero and Fray Gaspar Arzate, and the presentation of Father Don José de Setien for the consolidation of the sitios (*rancherías*).[23]

But this information does not fulfill or complete the objective of this book, which is only to present the island of Negros with perfect veracity and accuracy so he who has visited the Island may be able to say: "These facts and observations are true; the events are told as they happened. The customs, descriptions, and works presented appear real." He who has not stepped on its soil may obtain from this book the most exact and fair image of Negros.

---

[21]Father Concepcion's 14-volume work was published in Sampaloc, Manila, 1788-1792.

[22]The basic distinction for establishing provinces in the Philippines was whether the regions required civil or military administrations. *Alcaldes-mayores* governed the former category, while *corregidores* administered the latter type of province. Sometimes the *corregidor* of Negros was called, however, an *alcalde-mayor* when the Island was still a military district (Romero 1974: 22).

[23]A sitio is a small cluster of houses, while most barrios (villages) are composed of two or more sitios. See also Phelan (1959:124).

CHAPTER II

STATE OF THE ISLAND WHEN THE RECOLLECT FATHERS TOOK CHARGE IN 1894

In the year 1848, according to reviews, pamphlets, and other publications which have not been disputed or denied, "the island of Negros lacked agriculture, the principal element of wealth of this locality; the territory was immersed in scandalous misery, and it was called scandalous because this misery was the daughter of sloth."

Where there are two provinces today, in 1849 there were no municipalities, roads, buildings, or agriculture, and few people living in the Island. There were in that year the following towns:

TOWNS (*PUEBLOS*)	PARISHES	PARISH AND PRIESTS
East Coast:		
Dumaguete	Dumaguete	D. José Gorriz, Spanish priest
Sibulan	Sibulan	D. Alejandro, Filipino priest
Dauin	Dauin	D. Félix-Algeria, *idem.*
Tanjay	Tanjay	D. Juan Qumbo, *idem.*
Guiljuñgan	Mission	D. Alejandro, *idem.*
West Coast:		
Ilog	Ilog	D. Mariano Guiquin, *idem.*
Jimamaylan	Jimamaylan	D. José Ma. Pavon, *idem.*
Bago	Bago	D. Balbino Gonzaga, *idem.*
Bacolod	Bacolod	D. Roman Locsin, *idem.*
Silay	Silay	D. Eusebio Locsin, *idem.*
Ginigaran	Ginigaran	D. Isidro Piccio, *idem.*

On taking possession [of Negros] in 1849, the Recollect Fathers from then on administered the parishes of:

TOWNS (*PUEBLOS*)	PARISHES	PARISH AND PRIESTS
East Coast:		
Bacon[g]	Dumaguete	Fr. Bernardino Soriano, *ex-provincial*
Siaton	Dauin	Fr. Tomás Mezguita
Amblan	Tanjay	Fr. Ramón Cabas
West Coast:		
Kabankalan	Ilog	Fr. Andrés Cobo
Jimamaylan	Jimamaylan	Fr. Agustin Olmedillas

In the years prior to this time a Spanish priest named Father Setien was in charge of the parish of Dumaguete and the island of Siquijor. In charge of the parish of Tanjay was another Spanish priest named Barcamonte. Both priests, according to tradition, had been important persons in Spain.

In the year 1849 the island of Negros probably had in its territory some 30,000 people, according to summaries taken from the examination of documents acquired through the effort of patience. Not one document worthy of faith and credit exists. These summaries were made years later by burdensome and painstaking work which required sacrifice and sleepless nights.

All of the political power or influence and wealth of the Island were held by one or two *caciques*[24] in each town. They had a greater or lesser number of carabaos, some gold beads hung around their necks, and some sacks (*cavanes*)[25] of rice (scarcely the necessities to support their families). The houses in which they lived were made of thin walls of bamboo (*dindines*).[26]

Public buildings, which were the tribunals[27] and schools, if such names could be given to these structures by their appearance, were of nipa[28] and bamboo lashed together. The exceptions were those buildings in Dumaguete and Bacolod whose walls were made of *pampango* for protection.

The churches and parish houses (*casas parroquias*) were made from the same light materials of nipa and bamboo. However, those of Dumaguete had exterior walls of stone; nipa was used for roofing. In the other parishes of the Island the churches and public and private buildings were in the most backward state imaginable.

---

[24]Under the Spaniards local government was oligarchical rather than democratic. "Political office was monopolized by a small group of 'bosses' (*caciques*) in each community. Venality, widespread but petty, flourished. In the Hispanic world this system has become known as 'caciquism'" (Phelan 1959:127).

[25]A *cavan* of unhusked rice (*palay*) weighs 43 kilograms or is equal to 2.128 bushels. A *cavan* of clean (husked) rice weighs 57.7 kilograms.

[26]*Dindin(es)* or *pampango* refers to interior or exterior walls of woven bamboo splints in a wooden framework covered with a mixture of lime, sand, and water. See Glossary.

[27]The *tribunal* or *casa tribunal* was the residence of the chief magistrate of the town and also the local court (Cushner 1971:264).

[28]Nipa (*Nypa fruticans* Wurmb.) is a palm whose fronds are widely used in the Philippines for thatching and whose fermented sap makes a popular, mildly alcoholic, Filipino beverage called *tûba* (Brown 1957:316-27). For a detailed description of the use of nipa for thatching dwellings in southern Negros Oriental, see Hart 1959.

Communication among the towns was by footpaths originally used by deer. On the western coast the easiest and fastest route to follow was along the shoreline, through the twisted paths of the promotories of Tomonton, Cabuagao, Minuluan, Bago, and Ilog. One took advantage of low tide, and crossed the rivers when the currents were not strong. A small boat was used, lent by some fisherman if he happened to be around, or one waited hours and days until one was lucky enough to find a boat to cross the river.

If the state of the province was grievous with respect to the towns, buildings, roads, and agriculture, the moral and religious condition of the people was no better. Superstitions, witchcraft, crude habits, vice, crime, and laziness abounded.

The notion of *balos*[29] or revenge acquired such importance that if Filipinos were insulted or injured, there was no other law than the knife (*siantong*)[30] and spear. This condition gave the island of Negros the appearance of a population in a permanent state of war. Its inhabitants carried knives [and spears] everywhere they went except to church where the weapons were left at the entrance, leaning against the walls while the services lasted. These demonstrations of violence sometimes ended in the death of a family or of someone predisposed to commit blood crimes. Fortunately, this practice has vanished from the Island. It reappears only rarely and at times when the northeastern wind *heats the heads of the Filipinos*. Exerting an irresistible and depotic influence over them that lends itself ripe for study by criminologists knowledgeable about *amok* and other predispositions of the race "characteristic of a complete absence of motives that condition the crime."

HISTORICAL REVIEW: When the Recollect Fathers took charge of the island of Negros, Don Juan Doroteo[31] was the interim governor of the Island and was, at the same time, *gobernadorcillo* of

---

[29]*Balos* (*balus*) in Panayan means "answer, reply, rejoinder, response, retort, return, reward" (Kaufmann n.d.:94). In Cebuan *balus* means, in addition to reward or answer, to retaliate or strike back (Hermosisima and Lopez, 1966:52).

[30]*Siantong* is a knife with a slightly curved point and a straight, longer blade than the ordinary bolo or *binañgon* (Kaufmann n.d.:833).

[31]Doroteo y Marigoy is not listed as a governor of Negros by Cuesta since he was only an acting official for less than a year (1974:141).

Jimamaylan. (At this time the capital of the province was in the town of Jimamaylan.)[32] He was a Filipino, a respected person of importance, who took over the governorship when governor Don José Saenz de Vizmanos[33] suddenly died.

Señor Don Manuel Valdivieso Morquecho,[34] a much esteemed official, took possession of the government of the Island in 1849. With the previous verbal approval of the Governor-General, Señor Clavería,[35] Don Morquecho made Bacolod the capital. He initiated, within a short time of his administration, a series of reforms, activities, and improvements that made possible what today is the exuberant island of Negros.

Señor Morquecho was an energetic, intelligent, and active man of strong character and zealous authority. In spite of being seventy years old he was able to carry out difficult enterprises. This gentleman protected the first Recollects who were the founders of the towns of the island of Negros. He unconditionally helped them in everything. During his administration the Island was politically subdivided into towns (*pueblos*), barrios, and *visitas*,[36] all which exist today.

He began drawing up the articles of incorporation of the towns and parishes, eventually bringing under these towns a large number of houses scattered through forests and fields. He gave these new towns, villages, and settlements Spanish names--such as Toboso, Salamanca, Lemery, Escalante, Argüelles, Magallanes, Marianas, Cádiz Nuevo, Cádix Viejo, Toreno, Murcia, Granada, Numancia, Jovellanos, Valladolid, Madrigal (now San Enrique), Simancas (now La Carlota), Pontevedra, Miranda, Isabela, Campomanes, Tolón[g], Zamboanguita, and Valencia. All of this was done at the initiative of Senor Morquecho and by the great and tiring work of the Recollect Fathers.

---

[32]Under the initiative of Governor-General Don Manuel Gonzalez de Aguila, Jimamaylan [Himamaylan] was made the capital of Negros in 1795. In 1848 the capital was moved to Bacolod (Romero 1974:25).

[33]Vizmanos was governor of Negros from 1842 to 1848 (Cuesta 1974:141).

[34]Morquecho was governor of Negros from 1849 to 1855 (Cuesta 1974:141).

[35]Narciso Clavería y Zaldua was Governor-General of the Philippines from 1844 to 1849 (Maring and Maring 1973:3).

[36]Echaúz appears here to use *visita* to mean sitio. The Spaniards used *visita* as an ecclesiastical term for a community with a Catholic chapel served by a nonresident priest (Reed 1967:212). Today the chapel in a barrio may be called *visita* (*bisita*).

During Morquecho's administration, Father Fernando Cuenca made an expedition over Mount Tipasi to the eastern coast. Father Cuenca began and finished the construction of the road between Bacolod and Minuluan [Talisay] utilizing the old horse trail that once went to Mandalagan and Banago--places that formerly were quite insignificant but now are truly important haciendas.

Señor Morquecho was a decided partisan of agriculture who, after hearing the advice of the Recollect Fathers who were versed in soil selection and crop cultivation, ordered the first plantings of abaca, coffee, tobacco, and sugar cane.

Don Emilio Saravia,[37] the first political-military governor (*Gobernador Político-Militar*) of the island of Negros, succeeded the most worthily remembered Señor Morquecho. Don Emilio, more of a military man than a politician, had a violent character and spirited temperament. He had a great ability to command and move both Spaniards and Filipinos under him into action. Shaking the laziness from the workers, he made them work in the fields. He built streets in the towns and public buildings adequate for the times. He made roads of former pathways and put the towns in better communication with each other.

Don Emilio energetically began the forcible resettlement (*reducción*)[38] of the non-Christian runaways who had fled to the hills, and those whose ways of life were undesirable in villages. This great project failed for reasons beyond his will and control.

With all the acumen of his military genius he defended the towns from the invasions of the Moros. In his last exploit at sea against them in 1857 he sailed from Minuluan in one boat manned by eight soldiers from the *Tercios de Policía.*[39] He passed among seven Moro boats. He sank some, and by his courage and daring forced them to flee from the coast of Negros, never to return. To the attainment of this much desired tranquility the

---

[37]Saravia served from 1855 to 1857 (Cuesta 1974:142).

[38]*Reducción* was a 17th century project to move Filipinos living in scattered and isolated communities into one main community or "under the bells" of the local church. This resettlement of Filipinos was to make it easier to govern and Christianize the people and economically develop the Archipelago (Phelan 1959:46,49).

[39]The *Guardia Civil* was first established in Spain in 1844 and introduced to the Philippines in 1868. It became a functioning organization in the Archipelago four years later. In 1880 the first *Guardia Civil* units were sent to the Bisayas, replacing the *Tercios de Policía* as the sole military group designed to maintain law and order in the countryside (Grossman 1972:4).

Navy (*Marina de Guerra*) shared honors with such commanders as Malcampo, Machado, Uaredes, Barona, and others.

All the new settlements with the names of saints were founded under the administration of Señor Saravia: San Isidro, San Cárlos, San Joaquín, as well as Clavería, Calatrava, and others.

During his term the population of the Island started to increase owing to the immigration from the provinces of Panay (Antique and Cápiz) and Cebu. This was a population movement not only desirable but wisely planned. At the same time he invited back runaway Christians who had hidden in the mountains of Canlaon (or in the eastern and western regions) because of their misdeeds.

In 1856, the Illustrious Bishop of the Diocese of Cebu, Don Fray Romualdo Jimeno [Gimeno], in agreement with Señor Saravia, authorized the Very Reverend Father Fernando Cuenca, who was the administrator of the town of Minuluan, to lead an expedition to the mountains. (This town today has tramways for transporting cane, steam plows and powerful machines, but then had only a few houses and was just starting to cultivate coffee, abaca, and sugar.)

He started from the mountains of Minuluan in what today is the sitio of San Fernando, continuing toward the south. In this short distance he took a census of 6,000 families of mountaineers or a total of 20,000 persons. He conversed with them and named *tenientes* whom the people accepted.[40] They agreed to group together and live in places he would assign them. But his work did not stop there. While Governor Saravia crossed Mount Tipasi in twenty-four hours (a prodigious feat, indicative of his daring and enterprising spirit), Father Cuenca traveled to the barrios which today are the towns of Saravia, Victorias, Manapla, Sicaba, Cádiz, Marianas, Argüelles, Escalante, and Calatrava. In spite of a thousand obstacles, problems, and disappointments, he assigned *tenientes* to these villages, counted the inhabitants, and encouraged them to live in a normal way, united and willing to work and to defend themselves against the common enemy, the Moros of Mindanao.

The highly successful expeditions which Father Cuenca made in these times resulted in great benefits for the Catholic church and the Spanish government. In some of these expeditions (the most famous being that of Carolan) he was aided by his brothers

---

[40]It was not unusual for the parish priest to recommend or appoint local government officials. For further details see Corpuz (1957:118).

of the cloth. Father Fernando Cuenca and his conferees fulfilled their duty by going from village to village, from sitio to sitio, catechizing, teaching, and promoting the *reducción* Governor Saravia helped, protected, and sanctioned by his presence and favor all that was offered and all that was promised by them to the people.

Without financial reward, without compensation other than the love of a country that had given him birth, and his sacred obligation, Father Cuenca, now administrator of Sondol, appointed as *teniente*[41] of that same town one Calalas, the son of Cuantao, a local leader (*reyezuelo*)[42] of people living at the foothills of Canlaon. Calalas was baptized at the age of sixty with the secular priest Don Eusebio Locsin as sponsor (*padrino*) of the ceremony. He was then persuaded to marry and live with one of his women and to resettle all of his people in Puncian. This was a place located behind Mount Mambabuy, above the town of Murcia and north of the Caliban and Bago rivers.

In Mampunay, overlooking La Carlota, which is the second foothill of Canlaon, Cuenca appointed Casitoy as *teniente*. Here he saw Casitoy's daughter cured of malarial fever in the simplest and easiest manner. The *mediquillo*,[43] after making some exhortations and preparations pertaining to his profession as a sorcerer (*ababaylanada*), placed one of the sick girl's hands on her chest while he sucked the palm of her other hand. In that way, with the force of suction he was able, as he explained, to draw the disease out of the girl's body without fear of malignant humors, contagion or contamination.

In Buñgajin, which today is Castellana, Father Cuenca appointed Causa as *teniente*; in Baylan, Camaitis was so named; and in Tinongan and Calactcat, the *tenientes* were Sarincoy and Amaray. Father Cuenca baptized Amaray along with all of his

---

[41]The chief administrator of a *pueblo* was the *gobernadorcillo* (also known as *capitán municipal*). The *gobernadorcillo* had four lieutenants (*tenientes*) or deputies who assisted him; the chief deputy was called *gobernadorcillo*. Since the latter official was a Filipino, who often did not know Spanish, the *directorcillo* handled the paper work and other duties associated with the office (Corpuz 1957:113). Cushner reports that the *directorcillo* was an adviser to the *gobernadorcillo* and exerted enormous influence in town affairs (1971:264). With the Maura Law of 1893, a municipal council (*tribunal municipal*) was organized consisting of the *capitán* and his deputies.

[42]*Reyezuelo* (Sp. "Little King") is the term used by many early writers for a Filipino *datu* or chief, often in reference to Muslim Filipinos (Reed 1967:211).

[43]A *mediquillo* is "A simple practitioner with some notions of medical sciences. . .a little or petty physician" (Hart 1969: 13, footnote 7).

people, who numbered more than sixty adults, after their instruction in the faith by Father Agustin Olmedillas, the parish priest of Jimamaylan.

For the Carolans, he named Manyabog as *teniente*. He was the most important local leader of the entire range. How he became acquainted with Father Cuenca and Father José Martinez (now, unfortunately blind and retired in the Convento of Monteagudo in Spain) is worth the telling.

The priests were eager to meet and deal with Manyabog. He was a robust Filipino (*Natural*) of regular features known to be a brave and valiant man not only among his own people but also in the outlying areas he was accustomed to visit. After appointing the *tenientes* mentioned above, one afternoon the two priests rode out of Kabankalan on horseback. They reached the foot of the Carolan range where they had had their visit announced to Manyabog and found Manyabog's people fearful of an encounter. Since the leader did not have faith in the words of the priests, as evidence of their honor and good faith, they left their priestly robes with the people (*infieles*).[44] They promised to return to the same place the next day to get their habits. They did so and immediately after the priests had eaten in Kabankalan, they undertook their return journey. Arriving at Carolan, guided by two scouts, they entered a lovely valley with a wonderful waterfall some thirty *varas*[45] high and more than twenty *varas* wide that formed a beautiful place among the rocks, bushes, trees, and climbing vines.

There was Manyabog in the midst of about 100 non-Christians (*infieles*) armed with spears, *krises* (*crisis*), shields, *balaraos*,[46] and swords (*sables*) made of *palma brava*. The group formed a circle around the priests with their spears thrust in the ground. Manyabog, who stood in the center, welcomed the priests by saying: "Thanks be to God. You are welcome as friends and as family." As a sign of fraternity he took and sucked the hand of Father Cuenca until he drew blood. Manyabog asked Father Cuenca to do the same but he declined, not because of any scruples but because of his inability to suck forcibly since unaccustomed to this ritual.

The names of other governors who have ruled the province are repeated with true respect and affection. They, within their realm of activity, and the Recollect Fathers along with the Spaniards and Filipinos, within their respective spheres, have contributed

---

[44]In this paragraph Echaúz refers to Manyabog as *Natural* but to his followers as *infieles*. Since *Natural* means "native," the two terms are not necessarily contradictory. See footnote 13.

[45]One *vara* in Castile was .835 meters, but this measurement varied from province to province in Spain.

[46]*Balarao* (Pan.) is a stiletto, knife or dagger (Kaufmann n.d.:85).

to the development of agriculture adjusted to local conditions. They are making the island of Negros an inexhaustible mine to work and an emporium of wealth and happiness for tomorrow.

CHAPTER III

AGRICULTURE

Such an important source of wealth as agriculture was in a truly backward and rudimentary state in 1848. At this time the sugar industry and agriculture were barely known, while coffee and abaca production was unknown.

The vertical sugar mill made of *molave*[47] wood, processed the sugar cane three times, twice through the cylinders and once through the *suallo*.[48] These mills were used in Minuluan, Silay, Bacolod, and Bago. The chimneyless ovens, similar to those used for baking bread, furnished heat to one or two Chinese caldrons (*cauas*).[49] They produced the cheapest type of sugar (*azucar binagul*)[50] or *panocha*.[51] This sugar was packed in baskets (*liplip*)[52] made of a whole *burí* leaf sewed with rattan. The Chinese plow which "barely scratched the ground" was used to grow the produce. Montilla, in Bago, produced 1,000 *picos*[53] of sugar; Luzuriaga in Bacolod, 700;

---

[47]*Molave* (*Vitex parviflora* Jussieu) is one of the most widely used of Philippine woods (Brown 1967 3:435-37).

[48]The process is described in somewhat greater detail in Varona. The vertical crushers (made of *molave*) processed the cane three times. It was passed through the cylinders twice and once through the *suallo*. The juice flowed into one or two Chinese caldrons where it was heated over chimneyless ovens. "The sugar thus prepared was called *panocha*. The process for preserving and neutralizing the juice with lime was then unknown" (1938:20th installment).

[49]See Glossary.

[50]See Glossary. A cake of brown sugar in the shape of a half of a coconut shell (*bagúl*).

[51]*Panocha* (also *pinocha*) is a cake of brown sugar (Manila 1905 4:540).

[52]*Liplip* is a basket made of the fibers of the *burí* fronds (Kaufmann n.d.:505). The *burí* or *bulí* (*Corypha elata* Roxb.) palm has many uses. From its fronds are made sleeping mats and baskets of many shapes. Its fermented sap produces a mildly alcoholic beverage called *guhâng*. For additional details see Hart 1965a.

[53]A *pico* of sugar weighs 63.25 kilograms or about 130 pounds. However, the *pico* (*picul*) may vary in weight in different provinces (Manila 1905 4:447).

Gaston in Silay, 900; and Tia Sipa in Minuluan, 400. This was a sum total of 3,000 *picos*.

By 1854 the grandfather of the owner of what today is Hacienda Lupit in Bacolod, Don José Ruiz de Luzuriaga, perfected the ovens, inventing the one called *economico*.[54] It was later used by Don Agustín Montilla (May He Rest in Peace), one of the oldest farmers of the Island, on his Hacienda Constancia, now called Ubay.

Agriculture progressed in this manner, through the efforts of a very few persons, until an energetic, fighting, active, and resolute governor was supported by the establishment of the Recollects, seconded by some Spaniards and Filipinos, and by the presence at the port of Iloilo of the British Vice Consul, Don Nicholas Loney.[55] All joined to begin to prepare the Island for its later prosperity.

Their unity was without plan or agreement; each worked in his own circle of endeavor. Some were valiant and courageous as befitted the talents of the governor and the inspirer of the movement, Father Cuenca. Some were vacillating and doubtful as suited their fear and suspicion of entanglements which could bring ruin to their families. Some were bold and had great business acumen such as Mr. Loney. The results they achieved were astounding. It could not be believed if it were not for the incontrovertible evidence of their number.

The Filipino of this epoch was a trader of textiles by preference, registering at the customs house in Iloilo 133,000 pieces of

---

[54]"The first 'economical oven'. . .was a combination of the old and new in the sense that it was still fueled by burning dried cane fibers (*bagasse*), coconut husks or bamboo stalks but now included among its parts rollers made of iron and a small steam engine to replace draft animals. The name 'economico' may have come from the fact that this innovation required fewer hands to keep the machine going unlike the old one where three or four laborers were generally required" (Romero 1974:29). Romero adds that research in the Philippine National Archives disputes the claims of Echaúz and Varona that Luzuriaga was the first to use the *economico*. The records show ". . .instead that it was probably Ives Germain Gaston (or German Gaston) who installed the first 'horno economico' in Negros at his Hacienda Buen Retiro in 1846" (1974:29).

[55]Nicholas Loney was the first British Vice Consul for the port of Iloilo when it was opened to world trade in 1855. He was active in promoting the development of the sugar industry in Negros. See Romero 1974.

piña,[56] a product of the industry of the town of Molo [Panay].

The governor of the Island was Don Pedro de Beaumont,[57] an advocate of the progress and the prosperity of the province. People began to come to the Island, enterprising people who appreciated the efforts of Loney, Coscolluela, Gaston, Luzuriaga, Montilla, Pérez, Sotomayor, and others. Now mills with iron machinery were located in the haciendas of Buen Retiro, Constancia, Binalbagan and Lupit. Thanks to the care and attention of the owners of Jaro, Ledesma, Jalandoni, and Argüelles--and to Gaston in Guinalaran--the processing of sugar improved with the use of European caldrons, creating types 1, 2, and 3 which correspond to the 14 on the Dutch scale.[58] Orders for steam machines and plows were sent to Europe.

In a note taken from the British consulate, and in the writings of the time, as well as from hearsay (since in the official centers of Negros the termites have made rubbish of the archives), it is proven what value can be derived from intelligence well directed to a single end. Loney was a factor in the change. He made cash loans at eight percent interest, turning over mills and caldrons on long-term payments without any interest. He took trips to Negros where he established friendship with Recollect priests who were enthusiastic, zealous, and strongly attached to their province as well as possessed of surprising intuition. Other factors in the growth of Negros were the increasing number of Spanish personnel (from two to fourteen), and the immigration of Filipinos from Iloilo with families coming from Jaro, Molo, and Miagao, where they had been engaged in the textile trade, in which their great profits had been reduced by the competition of the Chinese. Land in Negros was cheap, from eight to sixteen pesos a *cavan*.[59] The continued presence of the Navy made the Moros avoid these regions. The price of sugar was good. All of these factors, along with the welcome, counsel, and direction given by the Recollects to both Filipinos and Spaniards, contributed to

---

[56]*Piña* is a delicate fabric woven from the fibers of the pineapple leaf.

[57]Pedro de Beaumont was a governor of Negros from 1857 to 1860 (Cuesta 1974:142).

[58]Sugar from Negros that was sold in Iloilo was classified as "Superior" or "Wet," according to whether it polarized above or below 80°. Superior sugar was subdivided as follows: No. 1, from 88.9° (or higher) to 87° inclusive, average, 88°; No., 2, from 86.9° to 85°, inclusive, average 86°; and No. 3, from 84.9° to 80°, inclusive, average, 82.5° (Walker 1910:109).

[59]In some parts of the rural Philippines the size of a field is estimated by the number of *cavanes* of rice or corn required to plant it.

the development and growth of Negros.

From 1859 to 1865--years which can be marked as covering the first giant step toward the agricultural progress of this province--there were 111,263 inhabitants supervised by twenty-seven Recollects and four secular priests. Twelve new towns were created.

The production of sugar rose from 3,000 to 40,000 *picos*. The price of sugar rose from two or two and one-half pesos per *pico* to three or three and one-half. If one added the premium on silver amounting to twenty-five percent (it is thirty-three percent today), this made a total of four pesos and two *reales fuertes*[60] or four pesos and three *reales fuertes* per *pico* if delivered in Iloilo. The cost of transportation from port to Manila was fifty centavos [per *pico*].

The first ship to carry sugar from Iloilo to a foreign country was the English brigantine *Pet* which arrived from Manila on March 2, 1859 and left for Australia on the fourteenth of the same month and year. From this date on, the exports to China, Great Britain, and Australia were as follows:

Year	*Tonnage*	*Country*
1859....	584	Australia
1860....	2,511	Australia
1861....	2,766	Australia
1862....	6,404	Australia
1863....	588	Great Britian
....	3,419	Australia
....	6,670	China

[Total 1863=10,677 tons]

A few more tons of sugar were exported to Manila.

During the years 1860 to 1861, the building of important haciendas began. For the first time, the whistle of a steam engine is heard on the island of Negros amid rejoicing by the Spaniards and some Filipinos at Hacienda San Ildefonso de Minuluan. At that solemn moment, the proprietor-farmer had around him, among others, government authorities who presided over the work festivities, and the Recollect priests who blessed the machinery.

[60]The basic monetary unit in the Philippines was the peso/*peso fuerte/duro* which was the Mexican silver dollar. A *real* or *real fuerte* was one-eighth (e.g., "pieces of eight") of the Mexican dollar or 0.125 or 6 1/4 American cents. The peso was roughly equivalent to the American dollar until about 1870 when its value rapidly fell. By 1900 the peso was worth only about fifty American cents.

The construction of irrigation canals was discussed among them. In close harmony and as one they also visited Constancia, Silay, Vista Alegre, and Helvecia in Bacolod, the first towns and sites to have sugar mills powered by steam.

Progress and improvement once begun did not stop. The first European plows came into use under the direction of Mascuñana, an intelligent, hard-working Spaniard. The task of producing sugar by centrifuge began at [Hacienda] San Ildefonso in Minuluan and at [Hacienda] Constancia in Bago.

Filipinos from Jaro and Molo came to Negros. Simeon Ledesma and Lucio Lacson settled in Minuluan where they laid out the boundaries of their properties. Ledesma and Cornelio Hilado created their wonderful Hacienda Bagacay. Lacson built the big and beautiful Hacienda Matabang. Haciendas at Binonga and many others were also established. Urged by the Recollects as well as by others, Coscolluela, Escamilla, Pérez, Sotomayor, and other Spaniards settled in Minuluan, Candaguit, Ginigaran, and Jimamaylan. They broke the ground and began the arduous agricultural labor aided by Filipino workers who had become a tradition that is still the object of admiration by foreigners and inhabitants of the islands.

Valladolid, once an immense forest inhabited only by some Negritos from Inampulugan, who had their huts in the place that is now the home of the heiress of Don Hugo Kok, became a town. Saravia, which was formerly a swamp known as Toc-gauan [Tokgauan], located between the Madalag Pequeño and Madalag Grande rivers, and frequently raided by Moros, became a town in 1860. It is today the location of thirty steam engines and eighty-four *molinos de sangre.*[61] Escalante and others enjoyed the same change. Everything progresses; land is surveyed, the boundaries marked, and then land is bought. As if by a miracle, haciendas and villages arise. The Island is in the midst of rapid progress, which begins to cause admiration, now that publicity has dissolved the shadows that covered Negros when it should have been known and praised.

From 1865 until now, the impulse given to agriculture, which began in 1850, continues. The exceptions are minor crises such as cholera epidemics, lowered sugar prices, a lack of labor, the withdrawal of credit, which had been liberally offered by two British banks in Iloilo, and other causes which the plantation owners on Negros have had to fight tooth and nail.

During this short time truly prodigious changes took place

---

[61]*Molino de sangre* or *maquina de sangre* were mills moved by work animals. The *molave* or stone mill rollers were operated by carabaos. *Sangre* refers to the animals operating the mill. It has been suggested this method of producing sugar was introduced in Negros by the Chinese (Romero 1974:27,46).

which brought about a revolution in labor techniques. Water-powered mills were built in Minuluan, Bago, Bacolod, La Carlota, and Granada.[62] Tramways passed through Ilog, Pontevedra, Minuluan, Saravia, La Carlota, Silay, and Bais. The steam plow was used in Minuluan, Pontevedra, Bago, and Binalbagan. European and American plows are used in all the haciendas. Irrigation channels are dug. The method of preparing the land for planting is improved; and the use of fertilizers is introduced. Barns and houses are roofed with galvanized iron as protection against fires, which can in a few hours destroy the savings of several years. Because of this forward thrust, the land near the coast is abandoned for sites in the interior of the Island. Within a few months La Isabela, Zarogoza, and Guimbalaon sprang up. The change continues to the Canlaon and Marapara mountains, their dense vegetation, a mighty barrier, torn and destroyed by the ax of the day laborer and the plow of enterprising farmers.

Religious and material improvements, however, do not stop here. Both Spaniards and Filipinos, in consonance with the patriotism and unselfish dedication of the Recollect priest, help him in his labors. Unimportant towns, towns paying small tribute, glory in their churches built of strong and durable materials. On festive occasions the altars are adorned in full splendor with images and ornaments brought expressly from Europe.

A problem well resolved yields the parish a goodly sum. A solemn baptism brings a gift of galvanized iron needed for the roofing of the church. Someone offers and grandly completes the renovation of the bell tower. Five crystal and bronze chandeliers adorn the apse. Building materials of nipa are replaced by stone and iron roofing. Cruciform churches begin their appearance. Small settlements follow the leadership of the parish priest. The churches of Bacolod, Minuluan, Silay, Valladolid, Ginigaran, and Pontevedra have been visible the last several years from the round-house of a boat crossing the channel that separates Iloilo from Negros. On the Island a superb clock high in the tower is a marvel. Churches are built which give renown to their builders. Spacious residences of the priest are beautifully detailed and elaborated. Cemeteries are under construction. And in all is seen the gratitude of the people to the poor Recollect who could have had much yet possessed nothing; a small tribute to his great sacrifice never rewarded or repaid.

---

[62]When Walker visited Negros in 1908-1909 he found that water-powered mills were limited to interior haciendas in Bago, La Carlota, etc., "where small mountain streams offered power enough to mill from 30 to 60 tons of cane per day" (1910:92).

CHAPTER IV

IMPROVEMENTS IN BUILDINGS AND CONSTRUCTIONS

Undeniably, building in general increases yearly, gaining in solidity, sanitation, and beauty. New towns, like the old ones, are administered by the Recollects. They have stone churches, some of which are partly built but already put to use, while others are completely finished. There are parish houses with stone or brick walls on the ground floor, and wood on the upper floor.

In most towns, schools and municipal halls (*tribunales*) are well-suited and spacious with plank floors raised about a meter above the ground. Some are roofed with galvanized iron sheets and others with nipa. Church towers are built of stone or wood with roofs of galvanized iron and have beautiful bells. Important private buildings such as houses of strong materials [wood or stone] or storehouses in all towns show a special care and taste in their construction, workmanship, and ornamentation.

In some haciendas, the houses are so well built and tastefully grouped together that a chief of the *Guardia Civil*[63] attempted to establish an outpost of that esteemed service in one particular hacienda because it looked so much like a town. It had a well-situated cemetery with small chapels, iron railings, stone walls, and well-made graves suitable to guard with proper respect the bodies of the departed.

All of these buildings have replaced the poor church and humble huts of the old town now improved with the proper planning and aligning of streets, well-designed plazas, and numerous houses properly distanced for public health. Most of the people live along the sides of the roads or streets which lead to the coast or the interior of the Island.

The needs of agriculture, given the distance between the haciendas and the towns, have led to the spontaneous development of villages or groups of houses. Some of them are important enough to have representatives of the authorities, who are

---

[63] See footnote 39.

sent to these far places to bring compliance with the orders of the *capitán municipal* [*gobernadorcillo*]. In such a village, the priest, to whose parish it belongs, has but a modest house and a humble chapel. A village can be converted into a town, with attractive houses, a well-kept church, and straight streets in a few months if official action to make it so comes to a quick completion. This has happened in La Isabela and Guimbalaon, and it will also happen in Zaragoza, San Fernando, Kabankalan, and elsewhere.

The old and new towns and villages have their own rights-of-way established by the government, by representation of each locality, and as imposed and sanctioned by custom because of the needs of transporation. These rights-of-way should be respected and verified so that they never give way to the imposition of the will of one or two individuals, protected by some legality, against the majority of the inhabitants of a town. This great work, carried out by an authority, active and zealous, will be of great help in avoiding disputes which, within a few years, will be of fearful consequences as property prices increase. It will become worse the day when the agricultural life of the Island directs itself to the development of the interior. This will leave the coastal towns as commercial and industrial centers, which will have a monopoly of the products, tools, and equipment indispensable for the orderly progress of those who move inland to work in the fields.

Data and Details that Prove the Statements of the Previous Chapters[64]

	1850	*1880*	*1893*
Inhabitants of the Island.......	30,000	200,000	320,000
Towns..........................	17	30	42
Filipino priests...............	11	2	--
Recollect priests..............	6	30	47
Wooden sugar mills[65]...........	7	--	--
Steam engines..................	0	59	274
Water-powered sugar mills.......	0	17	47
Animal-powered iron sugar mills.	0	495	500
Steam-powered plows............	0	0	3
Tramways.......................	0	0	23
Sugar (*picos*)..................	3,000	618,120	1,800,000
Rice (*cavanes*).................	10,000	659,330	430,000
Corn (*cavanes*)[66]...............	2,000	153,840	200,000
Tobacco (*fardos*[67] or bundles)...	1,000	4,827	6,317
Abaca (*picos*)..................	0	12,322	16,740
Coffee (*cavanes*)...............	0	4,298	1,115

[64]In the book these three years are presented as separate tables. These tables have been combined.

[65]For the years with 0, no entry was given by Echaúz. For entries with --, Echaúz used >> which means, in this case, none.

[66]A *cavan* of shelled corn weighs 58.5 kilograms.

[67]A *fardo* of tobacco weighs 14.6 kilograms.

New Towns with Churches

Made of stone, mortar or other strong materials and with a galvanized roof.

[*Towns*]	
Bacolod	Fray Mauricio Ferrero.
Silay	Fray Patricio Adell. Under construction but used for divine services.
Bago	Planned; materials being gathered.
Valladolid	Completed and built by Fray Carlos Ubeda.
San Enrique	Work completed by Fray Inocencio Sola.
Pontevedra	Work started and finished by Fray Andrés Ferrero.
Ginigaran	Work started and finished by Fray Francisco Ayarra.
La Carlota	Under construction, the work advances under Fray Andrés Torres.
Isabela	Under construction by Fray Mariano Lasa.
Jimamaylan	Walls of *pampango*[68] by Fray Pedro Sanz.
Kabankalan	Walls of *pampango* by Fray Joaquin Navarro.
Ilog	Walls of *pampango* by Don Mariano Guiquin and Fray Cándido Diez.
Cauayan	Walls of *pampango* by Fray Nicanor Arciniega and Fray Francisco Rada.
Saravia	Strong materials by Fray Hilarion Narra and Fray Francisco Rada.
Cádiz Nuevo	Being constructed by Fray Angel Belaza and Fray Blas Martinez.
Magallanes	Light materials [nipa and bamboo] by Fray Victoriano Tarazona.
Escalante	By Fray Ciriaco Echevarria.
Calatrava	By Fray Angel Maestro.
San Cárlos	By Fray Pedro Chivite.
Guiljuñgan	By Fray Angel Martinez.
Tayasan	By Fray Bernardino Remirez.
Manjuyod	By Fray Juan Zúñiga.
Bais	By Fray Guillermo Garcia.
Amblan	By Fray Matias Villamayor and successors.
Tanjay	By Fray Jorge Carcavilla and his successor, Fray Julian Adán.
Sibulan	By Fray Pedro Echevarria.
Dumaguete	By Fray Juan Félix and by the *Provincial* Fray Mariano Bernad, strong materials [wood and stone].

---

[68] See Glossary.

Bacon[g].................... By Fray Leandro Arrué who is today Bishop of Jaro, strong materials.
Zamboanguita................ By Fray Lorenzo Cordón.
Dauin....................... By Fray Tomás Gonzalez.
Siaton...................... By Fray Julian Adán, strong materials.
Bayauan [Bayawan, today Tolong]................... By Fray Angel Maestro.
Sumag....................... By Fray Severino Garijo.
Minuluan [Talisay].......... Under construction by Fray Fernando Cuenca, used for services.

These numbers and figures demonstrate tremendous efforts that include anxiety and hardship, continuous struggle, and countless difficulties. They illustrate economic need on one day, comfort and well-being on the next, lost projects, and unfulfilled dreams. Some people live in backwardness and misery, but a large number are progressive and happy. This book would be incomplete if it did not record the names of Spaniards and Filipinos, those sons of the plow and of labor--as they prided themselves to be known. It is a small tribute of gratitude so that their memory will not be forgotten by those who will come to enjoy and to collect the bountiful legacy they gave to the future.

Negros must never forget that in Pontevedra and La Carlota surnames like Frias, Urquijo, Gurrea, Camon, Uriarte, Perez, Locsin, Tejido, Zuloaga, Aldecoa, Lopátegui, Corteza, Araneta, and others are remembered with love and respect. In Ginigaran, the Colmenares, Sotomayor, Yulo, Sigüenza, Viña, and Pelayo. In Jimamaylan, Isabela and Kabankalan, the Nogueras, Lizárraga, Monton, Alvarez, Ramos, and Vidaurrázaga. In Minuluan, the Coscolluelas, Cuenca, Lacson, Ledesma, La Rama, Lizares, and Sison. In Bacolod, the Luzuriagas, Montelibano, Gonzaga, La Rama and Ramos. In Silay, the Lopezes, Ledesma, Locsin, Jarra, Hilado, Severino, Tarrosa, Hernaez, and Montinola. In Bago, the Montillas, Amonátegui, Araneta, and Amechazurra. In Saravia, the Azconas, Tongoy, Magalona, Gustilo, Benedicto, Ledesma, Maravilla, and Cuaycong. In Bais, the Montenegros, Avella, San Andrés, Gomez, and Diago. And in other places, the Cañete, Lasarte, Estebanez, Vega, Santua, Lerenas, Arenas, Tagle, Pastor, Basagoiti, and many others.

All of these persons are worthy of remembrance and deserving of the honor that, with the passage of time, in the new foundations that today are projected missions and tomorrow's towns, the great work they began be given due consideration. Their memory should be kept alive by giving the plazas their names that are a hundred times more pleasing to the ear than those that are of doubtful origin and unflattering to lovers of so generous and splendid a country.

CHAPTER V

HOW WORK IS DONE ON THE HACIENDAS

Agricultural work in Negros generally is not done directly by the owners of the haciendas. Rental agreements and management contracts are given for a flat fee in cash, a proportion of the production, through sharecropping (*acsas*)[69] or tenant farming. Tenant farming is the most common method varying with the financial situation and social position of the hacienda owner.

The method of the administration of the hacienda needs no explanation. A representative of the proprietor attends the property more or less with good attention, and sees to its needs with some goodwill. He receives for his work a monthly or annual salary. His income is increased with the sale of *anisado* [*aguardiente*, a locally made alcoholic liquor], cloth, tobacco, and other goods that the field hands are beginning to demand for their general comfort.

The leasing of land is little known. It results in extreme exploitation of the land by the renter and in undoubted injury to the interests of the proprietor. He often is in for a disappointment when, over the years, he sees the prosperity of the man to whom he rented the land. Sometimes the lease is made for new haciendas and the proprietor finds himself, at its termination, with an estate he did not expect.

Renting for a third, fourth, and even a fifth of the produce is frequent and both parties seem satisfied by the arrangement. These contracts have clauses demanding delivery of the produce to the nearest town, wharf, or in Iloilo. They may also contain clauses pertaining to the upkeep of buildings and the replacement of animals and equipment, as well as other clauses, more or less foresighted, depending on the sagacity of the parties to the contract.

---

[69]See Glossary. Under the *ascas* system "the owner of an hacienda supplied the laborers with the land, draft animals and ploughing implements. In turn the laborer took care of the cultivation and received as payment one-third of the value of the product, usually paid to him in cash. Although the expense for manufacturing was borne by the owner, in haciendas where iron mills existed, 9% to 12% was removed from the tenant's share as compensation to the owner" (Romero 1974:35-36).

Sharecropping is the best, easiest, and most convenient method. The hacienda with good sharecroppers develops steadily each day profiting more, and creating imperceptibly and painlessly a state of wealth for the owner. The owner gives the sharecropper a number of carabaos and land, and advances him money that he will repay in sugar at a relatively high interest. The sharecropper generally is a hardworking individual with some resources or a large family. The sharecropper remains tied to the proprietor because of the pecuniary loan, because they live on the same hacienda, and because of the need to mill the cane both of them grew in a common place. In times of great need the owner hastens to help with his animals and workers, an attention which usually is never forgotten by the sharecropper.

The sharecropper, as time and the years pass, develops an attachment and love for the place where he has his house, his sons have been born, and he has begun to prosper. Sometimes he helps the proprietor in kind and other times with money, gathering wood, consenting to cut and transport the sugar cane, and doing such things which make him an integral part of the hacienda.

The cultivation and work necessary to make the sugar cane yield its produce are not as simple as some think. This is no doubt the result of the lack of knowledge of the advanced state of agriculture in Negros.

In June, which can be considered the beginning of the agricultural year, work begins by preparing the new ground that will be planted in the following months.[70] The fields are plowed one, two, and even six times, then harrowed, leaving them ready to be planted with the cane points.[71] The points are fertilized and planted at a distance from each other so air may circulate freely and the work be done easily. The cultivated land is planted from September until March. When the cuttings sprout, they are carefully tended by weeding and plowing the soil between them without touching the roots to eradicate the weeds. The plants are gently cultivated with the plow two, three, four, and five times. The soil is also loosened with a hoe and later, once the plant sprouts, the earth is mounded around it with a shovel.

The field where the cane is planted is crossed by drainage ditches that carry away the excess waters of the northeast and

---

[70]For a detailed description of the preparation of the field, planting, and harvesting of sugar cane in the early 20th century in Negros see Walker 1910:82*ff*.

[71]The cane points (*puntas*) were the white tops (from twenty to twenty-five centimeters long) of the mature cane. They were cut while the cane stood or removed after the cane had been harvested (Walker 1910:83).

southwest monsoons whose force and continuous rain can ruin the cane. These ditches help the cane in the fight against its most dangerous enemy--excessive rain.

In a number of haciendas the recently planted cane, after being cut, grows what is locally called a *gala-anan* or bud. If tended with care the bud will improve the class of sugar, although it loses in quantity what it gains in quality.[72]

The plows used in Negros, sad it is to admit, come from England and America. It is the same with the spades and the *bagazo* [*bagasse* or sugar cane pulp] collecting equipment. The steam engine trademarks do not read "*Maquinista Terrestre y Marítima*" or "*Arsenal Civil de Barcelona*" because they do not come from Spain. All of them, without exception, are imported from England or the United States. One can say the same of the tramways (*tranvias*), galvanized iron sheets, sugar containers, oven doors, and furnaces.

Now that privileged Bilbao, with its blast furnaces and its *Vizcaya*, a great investment of Biscayan resources, seeks aid through a treaty which will soon have the force of an international contract and favored by rates and tariffs, she can look forward to a broad field, the handsome prospect of trade in the Philippines.[73]

Brother Spaniards, come to the Philippines, study, observe, construct more and more machines. Return importations to Spain and let Spanish trademarks be seen anew. Do not beg for protective trade privileges because you are in your own territory. Establish commercial and industrial relations that are indissoluble links of fraternity. Do away with the yoke of preferential treatment. At the same time that this trade gives life to your factories, it will render immense service to Spanish shipping in your parts and to these islands. These activities will create currents of imports and exports that will yield immense benefits to both Spain and the Archipelago.

---

[72]Some haciendas permitted the ratoons (sprouts of the cane after it has been cropped) to grow without replanting the fields with points. However, the amount of sugar produced by such cane gradually decreases (Walker 1910:85-86,88).

[73]Bilbao is a city and port in northern Spain, the capital of Biscay, one of the three provinces forming the Basque country. Here are located some of Spain's major heavy and chemical industries. Metallurgical industries predominate, based on iron ore located west of Bilbao.

Figure 3: Cleaning the weeds from the young sugar cane. (Walker)

Figure 4: Hauling the cut cane from the field to the mill. (Walker)

CHAPTER VI

SUPERSTITIONS AND CUSTOMS OF THE INHABITANTS OF THE ISLAND OF NEGROS WHEN THE RECOLLECT FATHERS ARRIVED

The superstitions of the Filipinos not yet converted to the Catholic religion are undeniable and common. Not all Filipinos within the Church have been able to free themselves from their origins. So many writers have dealt with this subject and have not hesitated to describe such curious and strange beliefs and cults that doubt often has been cast upon the truthfulness of what has been written. It is true that from the time of the rajahs of Colambu and Siagu,[74] of whom Pigafetta speaks, to the present, Filipinos have "adored hollow idols with hollow backs, crooked arms and legs, with feet turned upwards and large faces with teeth as big as those of the wild hog." So much has been written on this subject in pamphlets, newspapers, and books that it might be well to eliminate this chapter. But in so doing the meritorious work done by those charged with destroying these beliefs, acts and customs that tarnish the truth of our regligion would be forgotten.

The island of Negros had so few priests to teach non-Christian Filipinos the sacred precepts of our religion that it came to the attention of the Bishop of the Diocese of Cebu to which Negros belonged. Under the guidance of so few priests, such a large territory could not escape from believing in idols and in shamanistic nonsense created in the infirm, superstitious (*babaylanescas*) imagination of deceitful individuals inclined, here as there, to fool and seduce the unwary.

---

[74]Magellan sighted Samar March 16, 1521, Two days later, his expedition landed on Suluan, a small island off southeastern Samar. On March 28, they arrived at Limasawa where it was learned that this island was ruled by Rajah Kolambu. On Easter Sunday, the first Mass in the Philippines was held on Limasawa (Cushner 1971:17).

Tamáo, Ludid, Cama-Cama, Talayjang, Manleo, Mantió,[75] Múa, Taijo, and Mamao preoccupied the people of Negros. One, like the knight commander, Don Juan Tenorio,[76] could penetrate and pass through walls. The others possessed the power to change themselves into dogs, horses, chickens, five-year old children, giants of colossal height, reapers of rice, and many other disguises.[77] They were believed in only by sick minds whose grey matter barely had space in their narrow, depressed heads.

Superstitious rites, now fortunately forgotten completely, were practiced to plant and harvest rice. During the new moon of May or June, on the night before planting, rice would be toasted in a skillet, ground into a powder in a mortar, sugar added to it, and baked to make a sweet called *padúya*.[78] This sweet would be divided into twenty-four portions and placed on twenty-four pieces of banana leaf. The banana leaves with *padúya* were then put around the field as an offering to the spirits (*asuanes talunanon*) that protected the field so that the harvest would be abundant.

In the seed basket (*tabig*), aromatic and medicinal herbs grown among the bamboo, a wooden comb, and a palm fruit were mixed with seed rice so that the plants would be as abundant as the teeth of the comb, as strong as the palm tree, and have the efficacy of the herbs.[79] This process would be done with *pangas* rice, that is, the type of rice broadcast by throwing the seeds into the air.[80]

---

[75]*Manteu* (*Mantiw*) is a ghost of gigantic proportions or fearful aspects, a jinn. *Tamáo* (or *Tamá-o*) is a ghost believed to live in large trees or in the dense forest (Kaufmann n.d.:571, 896).

[76]*Don Juan Tenorio* was a play written by José Zorrilla y Moral, first produced in 1844 and staged in the Spanish speaking world on All Souls' Day (November 2nd). This gallant Spanish nobleman specialized in seducing women. Filipinos with the same alleged penchant often are jokingly referred to as Tenorio.

[77]Reference, most likely, is to the *asuwang* who is a man or woman with magical powers. See Lynch 1949.

[78]*Padúya* is a sweet made of rice flour mixed with sugar and shredded coconut (Kaufmann n.d.:633).

[79]Bisayan Filipino magic usually is the imitative variety in which one imitates the desired result.

[80]See Glossary.

The ceremonies of harvesting rice were no less curious. The night before the harvest, the owner would get seven *gantas*[81] of this cereal from the field to make *pilipig*, rice that was toasted and then pounded; *ubas*[82] which was a little greener than the ripe rice mentioned above, and *bayíbayí*.[83] The three were mixed with [grated] coconut meat, sugar was added, and a dough made that was pounded once more in the mortar.

When this preparation was ready the *babaylan* was called, a person that officiates at these superstitious rites, who makes the offering, yells like one possessed, skips, leaps, and foams at the mouth during the sacrifices and meetings held by the superstitious. He entered the house and stood in one of the rooms while smoke was made around him. He invoked the demons (*espiritus familiares*),[84] trembled ceaselessly, and recited prayers that were incomprehensible to all those present. This lasted from midnight until 4 a.m. when he would leave the house with the owner to go to the rice fields and distribute along the property line the dough made of rice flour, coconut and sugar. This was done so the spirits of the forest would not eat crops that were about to be harvested, and in this way the owner would have a better harvest. It was believed that a person who tasted the concoction spread in the field would certainly sicken and become gravely ill.

The people were no less imbued with superstitious apprehensions, counsels, and customs.

A pregnant woman, according to those believing in Manleo, Mantió, and Tamáo, should not leave the house or take a walk without a handkerchief around her shoulders.[85]

She should not walk over but under strung ropes or cords; otherwise the child would be born defective.

She should not wear a rosary around her neck lest the child be born with the umbilical cord [twisted tightly] around her neck.

---

[81]A *ganta* of unhusked rice is 1.72 kilograms; of clean rice, 2.3 kilograms.

[82]*Ubas* is "Very young, inmature rice prepared as food" (Kaufmann n.d.:974).

[83]*Bayíbayí* (or *baíbaí*) is a dish of pounded rice mixed with sugar and grated coconut (Kaufmann n.d.:115).

[84]This reference could be to either or both the ancestral spirits (*kalags*) or the environmental spirits (*ingkanto*).

[85]For a similar list of tabus observed by pregnant women in the Philippines, see Hart 1965b:42-47.

She should not eat boiled rice (*morisqueta*)[86] because the birth of the child will be dangerous.

No banana hand should be brought into the house of a pregnant woman.

There should be no talk about the hawk (*gabilan*) nor should the woman leave the house while this bird is in the vicinity.

She should not cover any bamboo container because the delivery of the child will be very difficult.

She should not rest on the stairs while ascending or descending.

Should she go into the forest or anywhere alone carrying rice, she should not eat all of it; she should keep some for her husband.

If delivery is difficult she should grab the handle of the bolo (*binañgon*).

She should not cover the child with black cloth. When he is baptized she would do well to have a banana and a fish called *lisa* in her hand to protect her child from certain contagious diseases.

During an eclipse, pregnant women should not look at the sun because the child would be born a harelip.

When planting a coconut tree, it would be well to plant it while carrying a child on one's shoulder. The tree will yield twice as many nuts if planted in this manner.

When one plants camote, as soon as everything is ready to begin the task, the workers should take off their shirts, lie on the ground, and roll over several times. Planting camotes should be done during the full moon.

If a wedding takes place and there is a celebration with much boiled rice and meat, the newlyweds are under the obligation of placing a spoon on a plateful of food. They must then take the plate to a corner of the house for the spirits of their dead grandparents to eat. If they do not do this they will surely have stomach aches.

Such beliefs, and many more, fill the imagination of the inhabitants of Negros, making of them a people who would trust everything to the spirits as if they were responsible for all the phenomena in nature.

---

[86] *Moriskêta* (Kaufmann n.d.:592) is the Panayan spelling.

Edward B. Tylor,[87] in one of his anthropological works, explains these absurd beliefs as emanating from the theory of the spirit, because the spirits "are considered like souls that exercise over nature an influence analogous to what the souls exercise over the human body. These spirits are those who produce the fire of volcanoes, those that raze forests in the hurricanes, those that make canoes spin in whirlpools, those that inhabit trees and make them grow. The primitive races not only speak of such spirits of nature, but treat them in a personal way which shows that they are modelled after the human being." The distinguished British anthropologist presents this as a general thesis without referring to any particular country or nation.

This is the way the Recollect Fathers found the majority of the inhabitants when they took possession of the island of Negros in [June 20] 1848. The people practiced those rites and customs that were embedded in their very nature. The work to be done had to be heavy and tiring at the start, so much so that an original and well-known case is that which happened to a young and energetic priest when he began building a church.

He had called together a few important people (*principales*) and a large number of laborers in the forest with the intention of cutting some trees to be used for the construction of a church. The work was begun with vigor; felling trees and destroying things is almost a mania with Filipino workers. But they refused to touch one tree [probably the *banyan*] that they said was the abode of spirits and, therefore, sacred. The Recollect priest, angered at their superstitious beliefs, took an ax and started to cut the tree. The *principales* followed his example until the tree was felled. The next day, no doubt because of the heat or some other cause, the priest appeared with a big boil on his face. For a long time afterward, the workers said the swelling, or boil, was a punishment of the gods of the forest. But he cut down more sacred trees and eradicated the superstition.

Today the descendants of these people go into the forest and cut any and all kinds of trees, plant sugar cane, rice, and root crops. If one of them still believes in *abusiones* or *busiserias* [omens or superstitions], words that have no equivalent in Spanish, they laugh at his expense and ridicule him adroitly. As anyone who knows and has dealt with the Filipino worker can attest, in *teasing*, in the estimation of others after his own fashion, and in the use of metaphorical language, the Filipino worker thinks himself *very* clever.

---

[87]Edward B. Tylor was a late 19th century British anthropologist who developed the theory of animism as the origin of religion in his *Primitive Culture* (first published in 1871).

CHAPTER VII

MILLING ON THE HACIENDAS OF THE ISLAND OF NEGROS

Agriculture on the island of Negros cannot be compared to agricultural activities in Spain. Here it has its own typical qualities. It is not the same as the harvest of the grape or the olive. It is not to be confused with the gathering of cereals or of other fruits, which create happiness for the farmer across the seas. It is the milling of cane, not its sowing, which is undoubtedly related to milling to bring chagrin to those who are dedicated to its cultivation and profit--that constitutes the only moment of satisfaction.

The poor and unhappy landholder is temporarily freed from the anxiety of devastations of typhoons and squalls (*collas*)[88] and soon to be released from the burden of the usurious loan (*alili*)[89] with its modest forty percent interest. For this, thanks is given to the stream of cane juice which comes rushing and foaming from the mill, to the iron caldrons close to the chimney of the furnace which thickens the juice as it is transferred from caldron to caldron until converted into sugar.

It is not yet dawn. It is three hours before daylight. In the barn or building where the cane is milled and its juice boiled, the first indications of work begin. The machine helper, or stoker, by the weak light of the coconut oil lantern, collects pieces of firewood that he throws into the furnace of the boiler. A sprinkling of kerosene or some embers kept from the night before ignite the fuel that boils the water and produces the steam. As soon as the gauge points to thirty or forty pounds of pressure, the whistle of the machine blows and the threshing of the canes on the tray (*bandeja*) of the mill is heard. The machinist awakes and the laborers (*panseadores*), who feed the cane into the mill rollers, take their places at the mill.

---

[88]Squalls that follow a typhoon.

[89]See Glossary. *Alili* is a "loan contract, the loan to be paid, mostly at usurious interest, in agricultural products; to borrow money on such a contract" (Kaufmann n.d.:26).

Some of the workers are surly, others sleepy. The rest are stretching themselves and cursing their fate and the early hour while they await the sacred word, the voice of the general of their division (for so the machinist thinks himself to be), the know-all (*aliste*) at whose signal pinions, pistons, gauges, balance wheels, and cylinders of the mill are set in motion.

Creakings, the hiss of steam, the tightening of screws, the lubrication of machinery, the shouts, and the orders of the machinist who, with hammer and wrench in hand, unhurriedly goes about, and the voices of those who feed the cane into the mill, are heard. A bell rings when the light of day first breaks preceded by a northeasterly breeze. All of these are the beginning of the daily work, carried out with such patience in the heat of the day that seems to glow in some ancient Viscayan forge.

The foreman, laborers, supervisors (*encargados*), and casual workers get up from their sleeping mats or from the ground and slowly go to answer the roll call (which is a necessary operation and gives positive results). One by one the workers are called. They answer "Present" and go to assembling groups according to the number of them on the hacienda. Later, the workers divide into crews that are assigned to undertake the different kinds of work of the day.

The plowmen go to the herd to get the carabaos that march at the pace of a turtle, as the earth is plowed. Those who carry the cut cane from the fields to the storehouse, collect the oxen and get the carts. The cart also serves as a cot where they doze during that part of a run when it is empty of cargo. Those who plant and those who weed have their hands in their pockets or carry a piece of cane or an iron stick. The happy ones, the contented ones, are those who, bolo in hand, must cut the cane, amid shouts of joy and of confusion which arise at the sight of a red-skirted woman who passes close to them.

In matters of work everywhere, in the tasks of the storehouse and the labors of the field, the foremen come and go giving imperious orders, always busy but doing nothing. But a foreman does not give the constant attention (with some exceptions) to detail that is required. He sometimes visits the house of a sharecropper or laborer where women live, with whom he can chat as long as he figures that his lord and master will not visit the vicinity.

At eight in the morning, the bell calls the field workers, who hurry to eat cooked rice with some dried fish, which will keep them alive until noon. The time from 8 a.m. to noon they help pass, combining work with pleasure; weeding and chewing cane, plowing and chewing *buyo*[90] or lighting a cigarette. Those who work in the storehouse eat there too, resting only a few minutes. They endure very hard work which is rewarded with two *reales fuertes* more than the salary of a field laborer. With slow and lazy steps the laborers return to work after breakfast, some to plant, others to their carabaos and plows, unhurrying and unanxious to please, but trying to do their duty. In these morning hours the hacienda presents its happiest appearance, just as it is at its noisiest in the afternoon.

Details, lightly sketched, show the manifold aspects of a morning on a hacienda in Negros. For instance, a long line of carts which, empty and loaded, move along the roads of the hacienda; a field where twenty or thirty workers animatedly cut cane. Other groups of twenty-five or thirty plow in the fields of young cane, urging on the carabao, by tugging at the cord which goes from the nose of the animal [where it is attached with a coconut shell button] to the hand of the plowman, or berating, or making urging nasal noises to which the patient carabao responds. There are those who are planting, and mill workers slowly carry to storage baskets filled with sugar. The whistle of the engine hurries the carts along. The activity of those who carry the cane to the mill is great. The sweet juice is clean. During its boiling, orders of "fire!" "even!" are heard. The iron caldron is full of foam and can barely hold the liquid. The syrup bubbles in the final caldron. The signal of completion is given. The heat of bellows cool the concoction. The sugar is weighed. And there is the *hacendero* who happily beholds his wealth. The sharecropper looks to his share of the sugar. The *maestrillo*,[91] with his slender stick held between thumb and forefinger, tests the state of the sugar cane juice. Another adds to the juice some coconut milk to moderate the smoke of the caldrons. One makes some sugar (*butong-butong*)[92] by hand. Cocks crow. The machinist gives his orders.

The chimneys of the machinery and the ovens still smoke. Their whistles continue to hail the sun soon to disappear behind the mangrove trees of the swamp not yet overcome by the evening star's burnished and shining silver light that rises above [Mount] Macauili. So, by the soft glow of sunset, the tillers of the soil work another hour.

---

[90]*Buyo* is a popular Filipino masticatory consisting of the leaf of the betel pepper vine and a piece of the nut of the betel palm. A lime paste, made from seashells, and sometimes a piece of tobacco, are added to the chew.

[91]*Maestrillo* generally was used to refer to the person in charge of making the sugar.

[92]See Glossary.

The carabaos return from the fields carrying the plows. The plowers sing monotonously to the beat of the slow march of the animals that have worked with them all day. *Bagasse* is piled up to be collected by carts that take it to the warehouse for fuel. The cart's raking mechanism drags along all that it meets on the path. The workers manning the gathering baskets (*punque*)[93] shout, and others answer. The rejoicing over the approaching end of thirteen hours of work enlivens the hacienda.

A bell, hanging on the porch of the landlord's house, rings out loud and clear. In the afternoon stillness it is heard afar. The noise and shouts are followed by silence as work stops. The foremen take off their hats, the workers hush, and they who were so noisy make the sign of the Cross on their faces and chests. The Angelus has sounded. They join in prayer to Her who is the Consolation of the unfortunate and the Mother of the afflicted. All kneel humbly, as humbly as the sun that dies and the star that is born in the great heavens where dwells the God of Redemption and Goodness.

Not one cloud mars the view of the pure, clear, blue sky. A single timid and faint star, of wavering and tremulous light--its luster dulled by the scant light of the brief tropical sunset--appears toward the Marapara. Then another one, more daring and shining, is seen above the trees which mark the limits of the hacienda from the sea. Many more stars appear and the vaulted sky dons its most beautiful jewels, its shining diamonds. Their light reaches the earth to announce the coming of a beautiful, sunny day never dreamed of by the hacienda owner, anxious to harvest the fruit of his vigilance and labor.

The *bagasse* has been collected and carried to the barn. By the light of the moon, workers eat a supper of rice, mongo beans, vegetables, and fish. From the steam engine, as if it were a farewell until the next day, comes a long whistle, signaling the end of work in the mill. From the iron caldrons comes the last batch for the cooler. In that part of the hacienda, before so full of life and noise, in a little while only a guard remains with his spear and two others with bolos (*siantong*). The alarm bell that marks the half hours and the voices of the guards who watch over corrals, barns, streets, and houses are heard.

A merry crowd has gathered in the house of the foreman, whose wife, a Filipina of pleasing features, is the Patti[94] of the region. She sweetly trills away and sings the songs of the Passion of Christ--according to her admirers--with sentiment and delicacy.

---

[93]See Glossary.

[94]Patti was Adela Juana Maria Patti (1843-1919), an internationally famous Spanish opera singer.

Figure 5: Cutting the *puntas* from the cane. (Walker)

Figure 6: Removing the soil from around the roots of the young ratoons. (Walker)

Figure 7: Cutting the sugar cane in the field. (Walker)

Figure 8: Loading the sugar cane in the field on wagons. (Walker)

The foreman's house is ordinary looking with a nipa and *cogon*[95] roof, *amacanes*[96] walls, and wooden posts. The bamboo floor is covered with palm mats (*petate*),[97] the carpet of the country. The parlor, the best room in the house, has three windows. On a corner table stands a little statue of a beardless St. Roque with his hound that looks more like an alligator than a dog. There is a statue of the Sorrowful Mother with a face gayer than a pair of castanets. Another statue of St. Vincent is a badly made carving of the hacienda carpenter who repairs the carts. On the walls hang inexpensive religious oleographs of garish colors. There are sleeping mats, bundles of pillows, benches, and chairs carelessly scattered about. Lying about are two books printed in Bisayan. The first page of one book read "The History of the Passions of Our Dear Lord" ("*Casaysayan sang mahal ñga Pasión ni Jesucristo*").[98] Other articles seen are a glass of coconut oil, probably more water than oil, with a wick, a large guitar, and a harp. There are many men, a good number of women, *amarradillo*[99] tobacco to smoke, and betel nut to chew. Conversation flows, everything is commented upon, important news is discussed, while disputes are avoided because of the solemnity of the occasion. People whisper of things that do not matter to them in the least, satisfying in this manner one of their predominant vices which is concern with things that are none of their business.

Women in tight, wraparound, dark colored skirts, accompanied by men who always walk at a distance ahead or behind them, depending on whether they are married or courting, walk quickly to the foreman's house, unwilling to miss a moment of what already has shown signs of being a great feast.

A woman, the wife of a sharecropper, whose voice, as someone has said more in poetry than in truth, is not pure and silvery, attacks a song in tones so highly shrill and nasal that it seems that the voices of a cathedral contralto, a cicada, and a person

---

[95]*Cogon* (*Imperata cylindrica*) is a tall grass that when dry may be used to thatch roofs. Also see Glossary.

[96]*Amacanes* or *amâkan* is a woven bamboo matting used for walling, ceiling, drying rice or copra, etc. (Kaufmann n.d.:35).

[97]*Petate* (Sp.) is a sleeping mat made of woven *burî* leaves. The term in Cebuan and Panayan is *banîg* (Kaufmann n.d.:100).

[98]The *pasión* is a recounting of the life of Christ, particularly His crucifixion and resurrection, written in octosyllabic verse, five lines to a stanza (Eggan 1956 3:1103). Also see Glossary.

[99]A locally raised tobacco with a very pungent odor; also homemade cigars loosely rolled with leaves of this tobacco.

with nasal polyps had been combined.

After a short while the silence in the room is intense. All is hush, breaths are held so that the noise of a mosquito in the farthest corner could be heard. The prima donna of the hacienda is ready to sing her verses [of the *pasión*], accompanied by the harp. She is calm, with a shy, wry smile, characterstic of the Filipina when she wants to please. With a voice trembling because of the crowd, touched with emotion, she begins her stanza until her soft song captures the enthusiastic audience desirous of expressing their approval. The singer's voice gains volume and intensity and reaches its full force. Jesus travels from place to place. He goes to the palace of Pilate accompanied by the melody of the harp and the exceptional timbre of the voice with its admirable sonority. Meanwhile, some people go about, not minding what takes place in the parlor.

At ten in the evening the song of the *pasión* is at its climax. However, the old folks and some of the workers are asleep--some in the kitchen or in the parlor, resting from the effects of *tûba* and rum (*tanduay*).[100] These liquors, purchased on credit, have flowed lavishly during the three hours of rejoicing in the house of the foreman.

At midnight, as the light in the glass lamp sputters on contact with the water, sleep has called the *pasiónarios* [followers of the *pasión*], and the pillows are full of heads. A few couples remain awake. They go down the stairs on the way to their homes. Peace reigns all around. The sentinels patrol, ringing the bell to warn the unwary. The moon, guiding the walkers, disappears now and then, behind ashen clouds.

Two pairs of men from the *Guardia Civil* are leading two notorious criminals across the main street. They pass close to a dark place, a convenient hiding spot with a dense growth of bamboo, brush, bushes, trees, and leaves. It is a place suited for an ambush. On the river nearby is a boat and five people who wait and spy on the group. Suddenly, the crash of leaping bodies is heard. Shouts of "Stop!" "Help!" A fight occurs and four shots ring out. Two lifeless bodies fall to the ground. Men take to their heels and the noise of paddles as they slip and slap the water is heard as the boat quickly speeds away. The guards of the hacienda rush to the place where the shots were heard. More men of the *Guardia Civil* boldly advance. The criminals are dead. Society is avenged, public vengeance is satisfied, and the institution that defends people and protects their property has done its duty.

---

[100] See Glossary.

CHAPTER VIII

PATHS OF YESTERDAY

There was not a single road in Negros in 1850. At low tide the beach was the only straight and sure way to arrive at one's destination. However, the difference in time between thought and reality, depending on the condition of the sea, rivers and boats, was sometimes a matter of days. During these years there were no routes of communication or need for them since there were only official contacts between the capital of the Island and the towns. These dispatches were fulfilled by government or municipal employees, carrying orders or funds.

The opening of what is today called the common or main road (*calzada general*) of the Island--or the royal highway (*calle real*), the only one which almost completely parallels the sea--was begun in 1850 by a Recollect priest. People still living remember when communication between Bacolod and Minuluan was a narrow path that crossed parts of Mandalagan, Banago, and Matabang--today valuable haciendas.

Since this date [1850], at the same time that new towns were springing up as a result of the urgent need for the good organization and orderly programs for the new inhabitants arriving in Negros, the main road and those up the mountains or reaching the interior, were laid out with ropes, without the help of surveying instruments needed for so difficult a task. There were no skilled builders to supervise the construction of bridges of strong materials, a few of which are still found along the main road today.

The roads that were planned and opened were five fathoms (*brazas*) wide. Today they have grown narrower because of the covetousness of owners of lands that have been cultivated along their borders. This practice has diminished the good work done that was suitable at the time when these lands were unappreciated and of little value.

Large forests, immense swamps, and endless areas of *cogon* grass (*cogonales*)--whose beginnings and ends no one knew--once were what is now the main road of the Island. Given these conditions as well as the lack of superior scientific and skilled personnel, the work and harships suffered to plan and accomplish this task would have been insufficient. However, there were people of strong will who were willing to shoulder this responsibility that was of the greatest importance at the time when the agricultural development of the Island was beginning.

To build the roads, trees were marked with axes, stakes driven in some places, rocks placed in determined points, and excavations and ditches dug--all with patience and persistence. These labors were preceded by changes in the sites of several towns that required interminable discussions, expenditures of energy, and acts of caring appropriate to the times in which a supreme duty to the common and general good was imposed against the private interests of some individuals. Today we see these measures praised by the very same people who then criticized them. Today we see proper justice awarded to those who saw so clearly, to those who had no thought other than the growth and increasing progress of the province.

The main road of the island of Negros does not have the features of a perfect, finished work--those of a first class highway. Like all Philippine roads, its condition depends on the scarcity or abundance of rain. The rains--squally days upon days that seem without end--are the most reliable barometer to gauge the flow of traffic. These are sad and dark days of chilly humidity, the cause of many illnesses. Weeks of grayish and ashen clouds that hang like some enormous gauze between the man eager for light and brightness, and the sun, soul and life, memory and joy of the Spaniard used to basking daily in its warmth.

The main road of the Island was made by the hand of man which had neither stone, cement, nor gravel within reach. Its sole merit rests on its construction. Its maintenance depends on obligations and needs at the moment. Because it passes through haciendas, is used as the route for the harvest-laden carts, and for the passage of objects and tools indispensable for the running of the haciendas, it would seem that the farmer should be the first to be concerned in having the main road well cared for and maintained. But, such is not the case. Among the important reasons for this conduct, is the everlasting question of the fifteen days of personal labor[101] and of other causes which, however, are beyond the scope of this book.

---

[101]This reference to fifteen days of personal labor refers to the *polo* or *corvée*. Male Filipinos between sixteen and sixty years of age were required to give forty days of labor annually to the state. (This requirement was reduced to fifteen days by a reform degree in 1884.) They provided labor for such public works projects as the building and repair of roads, bridges, churches, etc., (Agoncillo and Guerrero 1973:96).

The structure and composition of the roadbed comes from the materials the worker has at hand. It is clay-like or sandy in some places, porous and volcanic in others. This produces lengths of one or two kilometers where one may travel from mudholes to flat stretches depending on the kind of earth over which the road passes. This makes for rare and extravagant journeys, which are a series of adventures, a Philippine odyssey that someone should describe sometime.

Traveling along the main road, after a firm portion, one finds a goodly stretch of mud and clay, and comes to an extensive mudhole made by the frequent passage of carts and carabaos. One must travel in a coach (*carroza*) because it is the only way to cover the distance separating these poor and good portions of the road. The coach looks like a kind of confessional, made of bamboo and woven bamboo mats with its latticed window covered by a piece of cloth. It is raised about two feet from the ground by means of pieces of wood which are called "shoes" (*zapatos*) or *batangas*.

It is a cool morning; the sun is barely up. The fields of rice and sugar cane are lush and green. The oriole or *tolijao* (*oropêndola*)[102] sings from tree to tree. The *doloridao* pierces the air with his sad harmonies. The *taguati*[103] repeats its name. The rice bird (*pitao*),[104] with many companions, flies in search of his own; he calls to them but does not find them. The imagination flies to many places at the contemplation of this panorama. The coach halts.

The carabao stops his march, impelled not by the beauty of the day, but guided by his unerring instinct, in times like this, by the sight of a huge hole filled with clay and water. Proceeding as the circumstances dictate, and with great caution, the carabao moves one big leg and returns it to the same place. He lifts another and puts it back again. Fear of the danger ahead and the choice of the best route perhaps occupies him while he rests for a few moments. He stretches forth a leg, then another. The mud reaches his knees, his belly, then the harness. The coach moves from port to starboard, from prow to stern. A corner sinks into the mud, then the coach rights itself majestically, and glides through this ocean of mud. Meanwhile, the traveler grabs and holds onto whatever is within his reach. The carabao's hooves make a *chac chac* sound as they enter the mud that spatters

---

[102] *Tolijao* or *tulihaw* is the golden oriole or loriot (Kaufmann n.d.:960).

[103] An unidentified small bird that is three or four inches in size and has yellow feathers.

[104] *Pitao* or *pitaw* is a "small bird" (Kaufmann n.d.:759).

on the traveler. The shouts of the driver and the creaking of the bamboo coach continue up to the end of the mudhole and the better portion of the road is reached.

If Negros is to acknowledge its history filled with honorable achievements in agriculture, it must face the problem of roads with determination. It must seriously consider the expenditure of large sums of money for the transportation of its products, becoming an example worthy of imitation by other islands that are in the same condition. It is sad to see on Negros' roads some twenty, thirty, or forty carabaos, taken from the fields, carrying only two *bayones* [sacks woven of *burí* leaves and rattan] of sugar weighing about seven *arrobas* [one *arroba* is 11.50 kilograms] from the haciendas to the town and returning with rice or other needs of the hacienda. This results in an expense or loss to the hacienda owner of two to three *reales* for every *pico*.

The towns and the farmers should not leave everything to governmental or official action. It is necessary that they unite and investigate the most desirable solutions to their problems. Should five farmers be asked, one by one, how much the transportation of his products costs him, each one would cite a shocking amount that certainly would not be excessive. Should these expenses be added, one can be assured that a well-built road or a tramway could be built that would save them both expenses and the use of too many carabaos.

To obtain this objective, one should begin by keeping the main road in strict and solid repair. Then roads leading to the interior or to the sea should be maintained, with good drainage ditches and a firm bed. Work should be done annually, if blessed with a favorable dry season, against the damage of the rainy season. If it is stormy, the damage done by the rains should be repaired, as much as possible, by daily and continued efforts.

The roads to the interior of Victorias, like those of Saravia and Silay, must be built on the routes of the old roads, with as little damage as possible to private interests. Where old roads do not exist, advantage should be taken of the level lands along the big and small rivers, taking, however, into account their courses and the extent and force of their floods.

Saravia and Silay should see to it that the routes to Kabankalan and Guimbalaon are kept in prompt repair. All obstacles should be overcome and the farmers should be encouraged to cooperate. Help that is compatible with an equitable and orderly distribution of labor for road maintenance should be given these towns.

Minulan [*sic*], Bacolod, Bago, San Enrique, La Carlota, La Isabela, and other towns in direct communication with each other, and also in contact with the interior--in some places to the foothills of Marapara and Canlaon--must gain the support of the uplanders and the lowlanders along the coastline. If these trends, scarcely begun today, which give to the towns various resources and guarantees, are exercised so as to promote the welfare of the localities, each one shall profit from its own sources of wealth and well-being. Each one must create its own fortune which through the network of agricultural, industrial, and commercial relations comes to be identical with the others and gives true participation to all who pay and contribute. In this manner, the spirit of absorption and centralism, which always had dire results for the towns, is banished. The most prosperous and vital towns are those with a better administration capable of independent actions, represented and financed by a correct budget that is an exact reflection of the happiness and the desire for propserity, the perfect portrait of the worth and initiative of their inhabitants.

CHAPTER IX

THE NATURE OF A HACIENDA IN THE PROVINCE OF NEGROS

A hacienda in Negros is an area of 100, 200, 400, or even 700 *hectares* [a *hectare* is 2.7 acres] of land, plowed, cultivated and worked by 70, 100, 200, or even 400 Bisayan workers who are under one or more Bisayan foremen. They, in turn, obey the overseers, some of whom are Filipinos. All of them are under the owner who sometimes lives on the hacienda and sometimes in the towns or cities (*ciudades*). This community produces 1,000 to 30,000 *picos* of sugar for a respectable total for Negros of 1,800,000 *picos*, thousands of *cavanes* of rice, and much abaca, coffee, and tobacco.

Within the hacienda boundary is the hacienda house, that is, the house of the owner or the overseer, and the dwellings of the foremen and workers who live with their families. There is a mill, other buildings for fuel and storage, a drying square (*plaza de asoleo*) where the *bagasse* is dried. There is also a place where the workers eat, corrals for the work animals, plus roads leading to the wharf, cane fields, towns, or the other haciendas.

The hacienda house varies according to the tastes, disposition, and income of its inhabitants. Sometimes an imposing building that may suggest comfort and spaciousness from the outside is drafty inside and the rooms are poorly partitioned. However, a house with a thatched roof and of modest construction may have an uncommon air of care and refinement, distinction and attractiveness when one walks up the stairs. But, yes, in any type of house, hospitality and generosity go hand in hand. Generally, hacienda houses are pleasant and comfortable.

The mill and its building often have galvanized iron roofs supported by rough wooden posts or strong supports. They bear the weight of a frame of wooden planks, sawed and cut in different shapes, lengths, and widths for the purpose of supporting the galvanized iron sheets. This building is the most important one in the hacienda. It contains the steam engine, the brass, steel, or iron caldrons placed over the oven, the sugar coolers, the evaporators, *clarificadoras*,[105] the mill itself, and an area reserved for the fuel used in the daily work.

The storehouse holds the processed sugar, rice for the workers and sharecroppers, and the hacienda's farm equipment. The fuel room holds the firewood for the engines and ovens and the residue of cane extracted [*bagasse*] from the mill.

The drying square is an area of ground that is clean, smooth, without weeds, and free of all objects. It is used to dry the *bagasse* until it is ready to fuel the ovens.[106] During the evening the tramway carts used on the hacienda are placed in the square while the mill is operating.

Life varies in these work centers according to the weather.

Is there rain?

Patience, farmers!

Once again the rain interrupts the work of field and mill. Once again roads are slippery and difficult. Once again works of construction and repair have become useless.

It is the month of January, according to the almanac, and there has been little planting. The seed is lost yet the wages are paid. The locust awaits patiently, sharpening its gnawing weapons for the dry season which God alone knows if it will ever come since the way things are going this year it will be a worthy fellow to the years 1883 and 1887. Rice rises in consumption and price. The little sugar processed remains in the warehouse because the heavy rains that paralyze all traffic have not permitted it to reach the market. The haciendas, which at about this time in past years, were happy and bustling with activity, seem like places of seclusion where silence and tranquility are the inseparable companions of sadness.

The Faura barometer, that little instrument whose black

---

[105]In a *muscovado* factory the clarifiers were settling tanks. In better equipped mills they might be steel circular tanks with steam coils at the bottom for heating the cane juice after liming, preparatory to subsiding the precipitated "mud."

[106]The fresh *bagasse*, after it was milled, was carried in baskets to the square where it was dried. It was raked from time to time to speed the drying process. Once dried it was stored in the *bagasse* shed for use as fuel. During the rainy season most mills were unable to operate on their stored dried *bagasse* and either shut down or burned wood that was more expensive (Walker 1910:93).

Figure 9: Exterior of a Negros Occidental *camarín*. (Walker)

Figure 10: Interior of mill, showing piled *bagasse* in background and the caldrons (*cauas*) where the sugar cane juice was boiled. (Walker)

arrow points to maximum and minimum readings, that apparatus which gladdens or throws one into despair, which warns and apprises, now never leaves the sign of "variable." Fixed, it neither rises nor falls from the apex but shows a large irregularity during the monsoons--the strong northeast in June and September and the calm in January.

Two snoring mastiffs, sated with boiled rice and meat without losing any of their ferocity and courage, lie with their heads resting on the floor boards. Their sleepy eyes, dull, blank and sad, and their listlessness so unlike their usual selves, acknowledge, like the lamb and sheep that lie motionless in the fields without moving or eating, stormy weather that prevails. The geese, those birds whose liver and feathers are so valued, and whose honking has been and is a signal of alarm to their owner and of warning if strangers come near the house, are still. Their long necks, turned like taffy twists (*tira-tira*),[107] are hidden under their wings, showing only their yellow, humped bills. Their strange posture foretells the little good the farmer can expect at the moment.

The workers' large hats (*salocot*),[108] and light shirts that adhere to their bodics, look like an old and badly thatched house with many leaks. Their pants, rolled up to the thigh, keep them clean of mud. Their arms, crossed the right over the left, tell of the cold they feel. The bolo, that has cut with one stroke after another hundreds of stalks of cane, is sheathed at the waist. The cane cutters walk home, preceded by one or another woman whose head is protected by a native red sarong-like skirt which is used as a raincoat. They go slowly, depressed and sorrowful, as if deprived of one of their most entertaining diversions.

The tramway cars, filled with cane, roll by. On them ride the drivers, silent and withdrawn. Only the *rum-rum* of the steel wheels rolling over the steel rails is heard. The quiet and melancholy•workers reach the warehouse silently without indulging in those jokes so common among them.

In the kitchen, the *flox sanctorum* of the Filipino worker, as the illustrious Father Agustino Calzado commented about someone else's kitchen, the workers are silent. They do not make lurid references about their food to the cook nor speak of the boiled rice and the lack of viands. They merely swallow more and more balls of rice, sip the broth of the vegetable dish,

---

[107] *Tira-tira* or *butong-butong* is taffy made of molasses (Kaufmann n.d.:160). Also see Glossary.

[108] *Salocot* is a locally made wide-brimmed hat, often woven from nipa leaves. Also see Glossary.

and eat the fish. They quickly go to wash their mouths at the nearest well and depart for work.

The rain continues. Rails loosen and car wheels touch the ground. The carabao stops moving. Neither the rattan whip lashing its back moves it, nor can the gutteral urgings of the driver incite it to pull more than it can. The flooded fields dishearten the plowman who returns home and deposits his equipment under his house.

The farmer goes to the warehouse. Surprised by the abundance of cane juice, he takes a bucket and fills it with juice. He places it on the graduated measuring scale and sees a reading of a mere six that saddens him. Boiling is slow. They do not stoke the oven with *bagasse* so esteemed because of its cheapness and the ease with which it burns but rather they use firewood. The foreman yells, the oven stoker (*fogonero*) obeys, and the sugar workers (*azucareros*)[109] listlessly move the skimmers (*espumaderas*) while the juice of the sugar cane runs without bubbling from caldron to caldron. The purifier smokes; the lye and coconut are added; the wondrous rod (*varilla*) is in someone's hand; there is the trough and cooler (*enfriadera*); the dark sticky liquid is difficult to solidify; the shovel and winnowing fork (*bievla*)[110] stir it, and the disagreeable grimace of the knowledgeable, is seen. All these indicate that the production of a common sugar is deficient of some element of sufficient exposure to the drying sun during better weather conditions.

The rain falls persistently. The wind abates, the omens are bad, and the barometer begins to fall. Milling stops. The wind turns from the first to the fourth quadrant, a wind that is known as *canauay*[111] in these islands and also by an epithet or qualifier that is very offensive. It is the harbinger of the *baguios* or *ciclones* (typhoons).

The clouds spewing water and the heightening wind battle contentiously. Within a few moments the small rivers have swollen. The trees reel and bend their branches and tops. The workers protect their houses. The hacienda carpenters prepare ropes and put restraining boards over the joints of the roof sheets of the house and storehouses. The orders of the cautious

---

[109] *Azucareros* were men who worked around the sugar driers. These driers were wooden tables about six by ten feet in area with one-foot side boards. The table surface was about two feet above the ground. On these tables the sugar was dried and pulverized before bagging in one *picul* woven palm sacks.

[110] Also known as *punke* or wooden rake.

[111] *Canauay* or *kanáway*, a northwest wind (Kaufmann n.d.:390).

owner spur on the workers and the foremen who obey at the risk of their lives. A distant rumble, an approaching din, warns of the danger. Water and wind respect nothing, flooding waterways, razing fields, uprooting trees, destroying houses and storehouses, sweeping away people and animals, and leaving behind death, affliction, and sorrow.

The flood comes upon a field, then upon another one. Soon, it isolates a house. The corrals are flooded and efforts to save the carabaos are great. The water flows with violent force through the warehouses. In some flooded fields only the cane flowers are visible. Bridges are destroyed by the force of the water. Boats (*barotos*), rowed by foremen and workers move from place to place to rescue people calling for help. A horse, fearfully stamps in its stall at the impending danger. Heralded by these sad occurrences and the cries of the endangered, is the ruin, the desolation and loss befallen in only four hours of what had taken years of sacrifices to achieve.

Has the good weather arrived?

The sun rises radiantly, splendidly, and filled with majesty, between the two sharp peaks of Macauili. Not a cloud mars its perfection; unencumbered, it rises worthy of great homage. Its ascent above the mountain is a triumphal march, watched by thousands who devotedly greet it. What a handsome spectacle! Never has the sun been more glorious and resplendent, never more extolled and hallowed.

The sun's light gives life and incites the farmer to begin work. Its warmth gives him countless bounties, it mends the roads, makes the plants grow, dries the *bagasse*, and facilitates the rapid cooking of the cane juice.

The cane is felled at a stroke; two or three more strokes trims it. The man who cuts the cane tops also helps the cart driver who gathers the cane and transports it. One, eight, ten, or thirty American plows, the hoe, the shovel, the fertilizer, the weeding, and the foreman who commands and gives orders to activate the hacienda. The drying square and the roads are filled with *bagasse* that, thanks to the heat of the sun, will soon become fuel.

Following the direction of the smoking top of Canlaon, the volcano that keeps in its entrails the security of the people of Negros, the chimneys of the ovens and the engines emit columns of smoke of varied colors, according to whether the fuel is the

Figure 11: Filipinos pushing tramway cars from the field loaded with cut sugar cane. (Walker)

Figure 12: Boiling sugar cane juice, showing skimmers (*espumaderas*) and stacked *bagasse* for furnaces. (Walker)

wood of the *pagatpat*,[112] *bacjao*, or *bagasse*.[113]

Rejoicing prevails anew. The cane juice measures a high of ten degrees, the liquid in the cooler foams and mixes easily, producing Number One sugar, golden, dry, and loose.

The feeders of the mill ask for cane; the mill does not cease swallowing the canes and the engine runs smoothly. The caldrons are filled with juice and foam. The bell calls for lunch but the workers, seeing twelve more cars coming filled with cane, do not stop. The happy drivers talk and sing as if to make up for sadder and more tiring days.

---

[112]*Pagatpat* (*Sonneratia caseolaris* (Linn.) Engl.) and *bacjao* (*bacao?*, *Bruguiera* sp.), trees growing in the mangrove swamps, are widely used for fuel (Brown 1957:65,97). Also see Glossary.

[113]See Glossary.

CHAPTER X

OBSTACLES WHICH THE FARMERS MUST CONTEND WITH

(The following paragraphs speak of the majority and not the exceptions.)

The farmer of Negros has not yet achieved the comfort and monetary independence that is his main objective. Many times he seeks but, in general, he cannot find financial help. To find help he must go through insurmountable difficulties or assistance is granted under the Caudian yoke.[114] Only loans by *alili*, with interest from fifteen to twenty percent, or some other usurious manner of borrowing are available. It is in these forms that loans, so indispensible to agricultural life, are assured safe and good returns to the Filipino lenders.

The hacienda owner struggles to work against obstacles inherent in the soil on which he walks. He faces difficulties originating from decrees, either mitigated or revoked, resulting from their interpretation according to the criteria of the interpreter by which he is always held in check, always menaced. Such restraints persist unless those on high give him some attention, not to grant unasked favors but rather to give him justice, more than anything else, in the matter of daily wages. This year a dreaded crisis over wages will arise if the harvest remains at the level of the past years.

The greatest enemies of the farmer are the rains and the locust. From the former he tries to defend himself by draining, making embankments and culverts in the fields that otherwise may be useless should it rain for months and months. From the locust he protects himself through perseverance and hard work, organizing the workers, and sending them to the places invaded without considering the hours of work or the obstacles to be faced.

He who lives on a hacienda struggles against the custom

---

[114] *Horcas caudinas* is a reference to Caudio, a narrow road at the edge of a precipice, where the Roman army in defeat was required to pass beneath a yoke.

of *tara* [a European commercial practice in which part of the product shipped is deducted by the buyer in payment for packing] which lessens some of his produce sent to the export market. No reason upholds this custom, neither does any motive justify it, unless it is the farmer who complacently accepts it for the manifest benefit of the buyer.

He is also up against a tax imposed by law on owning mills, although the mills are indispensable if the cultivated and harvested cane is to be processed for sale. The hacienda owner, because of the harsh and commanding ways of custom which are more forceful than sanctioned and published laws, and because of his lack of capital, is both a tiller of the soil and an industrialist. He cultivates and endeavors to produce sugar by quick and simple methods. Both the fieldwork and the processing of sugar occur simultaneously during some months of the year, so that he is forced to spend large sums of money. He often is a victim of usury for there is no other way for him to obtain funds. Until central processing plants are established that would let the farmer be a farmer and the manufacturer a manufacturer, the hacienda owner will not prosper as he should in spite of the fertility of the soil, the low cost of field labor, and the yields obtained when compared with the amounts produced in Spain.

These obstacles are minor when compared with the greatest problem of all, the problem that hurts him most. This problem will end agriculture in Negros if some drastic action is not taken or a law is not passed applicable to all. This is the problem of daily wages.

Negros, presently under intensive cultivation that increases daily, needs daily laborers. There are sufficient laborers on the Island, but they do not like daily work in the fields. They prefer to enjoy the bounties of the plains and mountains laden with fruit or the resources of the rivers and seas that, with little effort, provide them with their daily bread. The need for able hands in Negros can only be answered by seeking them in other provinces.

September arrives and the farmer beholds and admires a good crop. His pleasure is boundless and he thinks, as he surveys his fields, of the *picos* he is going to harvest. But amidst his satisfaction an uneasiness plagues him, one thought worries him--the need for laborers. To calm these fears, he sends 30,000 or 40,000 pesos to the island of Panay. November comes, December comes, and January passes. Yet, the contract for which the money was paid is not fulfilled. Neither the number of workers agreed upon arrives at the hacienda, nor is the money paid in advance returned to the owner.

Twenty or thirty men, with their small bundles of clothing, present themselves at the mill. They speak to the foreman expressing their willingness to work because they know the hacienda owner is kind and treats his workers well. Finally, after much bargaining, they set the rate of seven or ten pesos per person which covers the cost of permits, two weeks of labor, the commission apportioned to their group leader, and the needs of their families. The hacienda owner sees the heavens open, and he deludes himself with great expectations with the arrival of help. The money is handed over. But his surprise is great on the following day when he finds himself without the workers and the money because the men had fled during the night.

Things like this happen today in Negros. It is necessary and urgent to find a prompt and efficient remedy for this evil which, if it spreads, can put an end to the work of many years. Stipulations with respect to hours of work, salaries to be earned, meals, travel, and the length of stay in each hacienda should be established. But at the same time, as part of the contractual obligations, guarantees should be given to capital and security of the owner. Bodies should also be created to oversee labor, and regulations should be established for this Archipelago like those of one of the Antilles. A law ending vagrancy should be made. And when the missions will be established, the missionaries and the appointed authorities should be given extraordinary powers over matters which affect *sacadas*[115] and vagrants.

Neither an apology in favor of the Island worker nor a diatribe to stress the bad reputation the worker has for laziness and corruptness is here intended. After all, where there are many, all types are found. There is no claim to follow the ideas of this or that person, or those of one or another individual. In this specific case, like others in general, the saying that each one speaks of the fair according to what he saw there, has exact application.

The insular worker of the island of Negros, he alone, without the help of outsiders, plows, fertilizes, sows, cultivates, and works to produce 1,800,000 *picos* of sugar and more then 400,000 *cavanes* of rice, and many *quintales*[116] of coffee and abaca. He grows root crops and clears the forest, leaving hundreds of *hectares*

---

[115]Echaúz uses *indocumentados* to refer to those Filipinos, usually migratory workers from Panay, who lacked proper registration officially permitting them to leave their communities. At this time Filipinos who wished to come to Negros to work on a hacienda had to obtain written permission from their village leader, the local priest, and the *gobernadorcillo*. This system ". . .made it difficult for the Negros planter to secure much needed laborers from Panay" (Romero 1974:38). *Indocumentado* has been translated as *sacada*, the term used today for migratory workers in Negros' sugar fields (Ledesma and others 1971:19*ff*).

[116]One *quintal* equals 100 pounds.

of land ready for agriculture. The mill represents sixteen hours of work. The fieldwork in scorching sun and unbearable heat fills twelve hours. With very rare exceptions, those in charge of the machines, the foremen supervising the storehouses and the weighings, are Filipinos.

The Filipino, united and directed by the Spaniard, be it in the forts (*cottas*) of Jolo as well as the fortresses of Maibung, or setting up new haciendas in Negros or clearing the forest, is courageous, active, and industrious. It matters not to him that this "*climate of fire turns blood to water and suffocates thought.*"

CHAPTER XI

WATER-POWERED MILLS [AND DAMS]

Perhaps the greatest of the agricultural advances of the island of Negros consisted in the construction of the economical water-powered mills, machines that saved expensive fuel and costly machinery.

Minuluan [Talisay], a town that in 1850 had only five houses, was founded in 1788 by twenty-two families who had escaped from the Moro invasion of Toc-gauan (Saravia). In 1881 it was destined to have the first steam plow in its area as it had the first machine powered by water.

It was 1872, and Señor Masgrao,[117] a defender of agricultural interests, was the governor of the Island. A Spaniard tried to install a water-powered mill in Kandaguit (a part of Minuluan) but the attempt failed.

In his visits to the haciendas, barrios, and rivers of Minuluan, Father Fernando Cuenca had observed with admiration and regret the course and height of the Imbang river and the relatively low position of the town that made it capable of being irrigated by it. His agricultural instincts were also grieved to see such a wealth of water flowing to the sea without being of advantage to anybody.

Father Cuenca, a solitary spirit, knows how to invent. He makes things, but he tells no one about his projects, uncertain of their outcome, until he has bridged the gap between the idea and its reality. Once his objective is attained, he turns it over to others so that they may use it and obtain the benefit of many days of experiment and some sleepless nights of thought.

The method he used to make the dike needed to hold back the water was very simple since it required only the materials and

---

[117]Cuesta indicates that the first name of Masgrao is unknown as is the date he became governor; his term may have ended in 1873. In this year Federico Lemery became governor of Negros (1974:142).

tools that he had at hand or could easily obtain. First, he studied the terrain and then, with sixty workers, and in twelve hours, he contained the flow of water. The water was held back by a stone wall that from a thick base tapered to the top on one side. In this way he made several reservoirs which slowed down the flow of the current. With stones and gravel from the river, he made the dike and towards the end, along the river bank, a floodgate opening into a ditch that would lead the water to fall on the millwheel. After a successful trial in which the power of the water was shown strong enough, the rest of the project was easy.

On the ground floor of the priest's residence, and with some workers whom he had trained to be carpenters, Father Cuenca first drew the model of the machine on the earth. He made foundry patterns, turned blacksmith, forged and formed the wheel. While making the wheel he also worked as a mason and with some of his workers constructed the containing walls of the ditch for the water fall.

In July of 1873, the road to the interior of Minuluan was too narrow for oxcarts, carriages, and horses. The governor of the province, the mayor, Spaniards and Filipinos from Bacolod, Silay, Minuluan, and del Sur, were gathered in front of the warehouse. Before them, beside objects of worship of our religion, was a wooden wheel which most people did not know what it was for. Father Mauricio Ferrero,[118] beaming with pride and accompanied by Father Cuenca, now dressed as a priest, prayed and blessed the wheel. A Spaniard, Don Diego de la Viña,[119] started the wheel by letting a great quantity of water fall in it, diverted from the Imbang river. Those were moments of enthusiasm, satisfaction, and gladness.

An enterprising man whose similar attempt in Kandaguit had

---

[118]During the Filipino revolution, both Fathers Ferrero and Cuenca were placed under house arrest. "In the case of Fr. Ferrero and Fr. Cuenca, the special reason was that influential citizens of Bacolod and Talisay endeavored to protect their respective *curas* from falling into the hands of revolutionists, even going to the extent of hiding them for a while" (Romero 1974:113).

[119]Don Diego de la Viña was "perhaps the most powerful *cacique* of Negros Oriental" (Romero 1974:105). His father was a Spaniard and his mother was a Filipina from the Binondo district of Manila. Diego de la Viña settled originally in Binalbagan "but a misunderstanding with the local *cura* led him to sell his lands to the Yulos and to pioneer in the wilderness of the Negros Oriental mountainsides. There he carved out a fortune in vast plantations that later spawned towns, starting with a lovely valley he aptly called 'Vallehermoso'" (Romero 1974:32-33, 105, 110).

Figure 13: The old--plowing the field with a carabao. (Walker)

Figure 14: The new--a steam-powered plow cultivating a cane field. (Walker)

failed, cried and embraced the victor of Minuluan. The authorities congratulated Father Cuenca. The Spaniards and Filipinos, united by sentiments of respect and gratitude, rendered congratulations to their best friend and protector. Since that day, attempts to install water-powered machines have not stopped; its first builder has taken a very active part in setting them up.

The advantages that the water-powered mill have given the people are many. It has saved them the purchase of choice firewood to produce the steam, and of many expensive parts of iron that compose a steam engine. It has also saved them from the fear of steam engine explosions and the wages of a machinist and of other workers.

Not only towns but also barrios have seen all the cane in their jurisdiction being milled in eight water-powered mills, one of them very powerful. Bacolod, La Carlota, Pontevedra, Granada, Minuluan, Silay, Bago, and Bais have in their jurisdiction such mills, some of them capable of milling 100 *picos* in twelve hours. The crude wooden wheel of simple connection has been substituted by the iron wheel brought from England and by the turbine that uses less water and provides increased power.

CHAPTER XII

THE TOWN OF TODAY AND THOSE OF THE FUTURE

This chapter is concerned with matters that manifest and document the endeavors already described in this book. Guimbalaon and Zaragoza: their names alone bring evidence of superior accomplishments achieved in a few months, of invaluable generosity for the common good, of incomprehensible progress, and of beneficial foresight. Carolan, with its very fertile and productive valleys, hills and glens, promises a great future for the man who works there. For the growing of tobacco it is better than Isabela de Cagayan [in northern Luzon]. Its coffee and cacao is superior to that of Batangas [in southern Luzon] and Mindanao. It raises a higher grade of abaca than that of Albay [in southern Luzon] and its rice is comparable only to that of Valencia for the size of its grain and exquisite flavor.

Guimbalaon

Guimbalaon was one of the eleven missions proposed to His Excellency, the Governor-General of these Islands, in the project published in October 1889 by the Reverend Father Mauricio Ferrero, vicar of the Negros Occidental coast. It was a barrio of the town of Silay, being seventeen kilometers away from it. On the northern side was a forest where the barrio could extend its territory and jurisdiction. On the southern side the Najalinan river served as a boundary between Dos Hermanas mission and itself. The Macauili mountain was to the east and the town of Silay to the west.

This barrio is a favorite of astute farmers. It overlooks the haciendas of the towns of Minuluan, Silay, and Saravia and the harbor with boats from Iloilo and the coast of Panay. Its soil is first class, excellent for growing cane, coffee, and abaca. It is a very healthy place. There is a fountain in the center of the plaza [Silay or Guimbalaon?] with excellent water and four surrounding rivers, the Najalinan, Samuyao, Napilas, and Malisbog. This year the outlook is especially good because in the low coastal lands there has been too much rain for the cane to grow well and the harvest is insignificant. In Guimbalaon, the cane has grown and developed without being delayed or deterred in its growth or vigor by the rains.

In his several visits to Gimbalaon the Reverend Father Patricio Adell, priest of Silay, examined thoroughly the area where the barrio was located. Step by step he went into the forest. He sent a companion, a brother of the cloth, to the barrio in the modest role of a missionary. Father Adell desired the prosperity of Guimbalaon as much as the welfare of his own town. Last year, according to church statistics, there were 10,118 inhabitants, 61 marriages, 245 deaths, and 413 baptisms [in Gambalaon].

Farmers have not been indifferent to such important progress. Don Cornelio Hilado freely donated the land on which the town is located. Don Ramón, Don Melecio Severino (the latter *capitán municipal*), Don Quirino Gamboa, and others helped the Father in this fruitful work, now carried farther forward into the mountains. There they began to parley with the non-Christians and have established religious relations which end in baptisms and commercial relations which have brought the people to the market on set days. In short, a new barrio will be established in the mountains, a barrio which in a short time will be as highly valued as the town of Guimbalaon.

To prove that a barrio aspiring to become a mission in Negros can prosper, it is enough to add:

That on the 20th of October, 1889, the Reverend Father Patricio Adell made his first visit, in the company of the colonel of the *Guardia Civil* and his fellow priest, Father Fernando Cuenca, as well as important people from Silay and Minuluan:

> That the inhabitants of the barrio of Guimbalaon and some important people of Silay signed a petition on April 20, 1891, asking for a *gobernadorcillo*:
>
> > And that on the 13th day of May of 1891, the chapel, blessed with great pomp and solemnity, was transformed into a church; and in August of 1892, by order of Father Adell, Father Juan Manzanares went to the barrio which became a town (*pueblo*) July of the year 1893.[120]

Zaragoza

For some years a barrio near Canlaon mountain harbored people of evil habits, robbers by trade and malcreants by profession. They were defeated by a force of the *Guardia Civil* under the command of three Spanish sergeants. They left the barrio pacified.

---

[120]Echaúz gives the date of the founding of Guimbalaon as July, 1893. Cuesta (1974:143) states, however, that 1892 is the correct date.

By order of his superiors, a Recollect priest established himself there in the year 1892.

The barrio has some sixty houses. There is a *teniente*, subject to the authority of the town of Bago which is twenty-four kilometers away. The lands of the town of Bago border the barrio on the north and west. On the south are the lands of La Carlota and to the east is Canlaon.

The barrio is advantageously located at a stop-over point for the sick on their way to the healing waters of Mambucal, a place agreed to have caused prodigious cures. If it were to become a town it could count, from its beginning, apart from the parish of Bago, 10,230 inhabitants, 50 marriages, 150 deaths, and 250 births.

In its jurisdiction there are extremely important haciendas, some of which harvest [annually] 20,000 *picos* of sugar. The rivers which pass through the barrio power fourteen water-powered machines.

One who had seen and thought about this barrio over the years and returned to it today could not accurately guess, without taking into account the prosperity of Negros, how the presence of a priest of initiative, urged on by his fellows and supported by his parishioners, could finish such great work in so short a time. Shacks of meager value and fields of worthless *cogon* have changed into houses and working fields; these [houses] changed to storehouses and those [fields] became haciendas. Two swiftly flowing rivers are stayed in their courses, and diverted, carry their water to power machinery. The chapel is expanded into a church; the cart is replaced by the tramway. Everything prospers, and will prosper more, if these lines of advancement called "Frontier Missions," placed in the mountains, are tried and become a reality.

Carolan[121]

In the southern part of the island of Negros, in the foothills of Mount Carolan, is the town of Kabankalan, a vivid demonstration of the culture of a farming community. It is thirty kilometers from the base of the mountain. On the other side of the mountain lie the plateaus of Tayasan, Jimalalud, and Ayuñgon, places that shelter ignorance and error. In the northern part are

---

[121]Carolan is an isolated sitio along the Hilabangan river, a branch of the Ilog river, located between Kabankalan and Tayasan (in Negros Oriental Province). During the Spanish period, when Jimamaylan was the capital of Negros Occidental, the people used Carolan as a refuge when the Moros raided Ilog and Kabankalan. Today Carolan, unaccessible by car or bus, is a several hour walk from the nearest road. The population has dwindled to a few inhabitants, mostly Negritos and some Negrito/Spanish mestizos.

extensive lands which embrace the mountain range of Suay. In the south lies the Tipasi mountain range where beside virgin forests--trees with shrubs growing from their bases, parasites fed by the substance of so much and such great vegetation--run large and torrential rivers. These rivers lap the foothills of the mountains, the source of free-flowing torrents where, among ferns and spontaneously growing plants, pure and crystal waters spring forth.

To the sight of the visitor at Lapjan, the waters appear as a very high waterfall. After flowing gently through the tranquil esplanade of trees, plants, and cultivated lands, the water falls quickly and strikes large rocks and the earth. The spray created, hit by the rays of the sun, forms countless effects as the water plays capriciously. This vigorous flow of water comes to rest in a valley on whose hills grow pine and other trees suitable for construction.

The land that comprises the greatest portion of this territory is first class soil, exceeding all praise. Sugar cane could grow, and its cultivation would be easy and cheap in the plains. The tobacco now grown in the glens and valleys, agreeable sights which please and relax anyone who sees them for the first time, brings double the price of that of Barili in Cebu. Its cacao is more esteemed than that of Siquijor [an island off the east coast of Dumaguete]. The coffee and abaca planted and cultivated in a crude way by the non-Christians are much sought after today.

These fertile lands are inhabited by 14,000 to 15,000 non-Christians who live in rude houses made of *ticoy*,[122] the nipa of the mountains. They live in very small dispersed groups under the command of a *cabecillo* (leader), *reyezuelo*, or *cacique* who acts like a father to his people. They are, in their own way, obedient and submissive to their leaders. Unlike the hostile non-Christians of the northern part of Luzon, they are, by temperament, neither warlike nor provocative. They have a certain independence and do not recognize an absolute ruler to whom they must pay homage and respect.

The non-Christians who inhabit Carolan are of robust health and physically well-developed. They are peaceful if treated gently but brave to the extent of heroism if insulted or if one does violence to them. They have no idols or unique superstitions, but share those customs peculiar to the Bisayans who are followers of certain sects of *babaylanismo*. As no one else, the non-Christians of Carolan preserve the custom of *balos*[123] which consists of taking armed revenge, using the spear or bolo (*siantong*), against anyone

---

[122]*Ticoy* probably is *tikiu* (*Scirpus grossus* Linn. f), a coarse sedge used to make thick sleeping mats, thatch, etc., (Brown 1957 1:206).

[123]See footnote 29.

who has done them personal injury or killed member of their family. They also drive away the *dañgan* [*asuwang*?], the evil spirit that attacks pregnant women, by hitting a bolo near the house of this woman.

The people of Carolan, despite their lack of contact with these neighboring peoples, have a reputation among the non-Christians that is characterized by hospitality, valor, and impeccable conduct.

The town of San Juan de Ilog, some forty kilometers from Carolan, was attacked and sacked in 1727 by the Moros from Mindanao. As was the custom, the Moros spared no one; they attacked male or female without respect for religion, family, or home. The inhabitants, including 2,000 terrified people, a Dominican priest, and the municipal authorities, fled to the Carolan mountains. They explained the reason for their presence to the Carolanians [non-Christians] who, brave and hospitable, gave them whatever they had. They began defense preparations but these were not necessary because the Moros never went far from the seashore. There, guided by piratical instincts, they commit all kinds of atrocities.

The good conduct of the Carolanians is confirmed in testimony signed by the Dominican priest and town authorities and extended to them as a guarantee and credit. This document was carefully kept to show their sons and strangers. It was shown by Manyabog to two Recollect priests who visited there a few years ago.

In addition to their good qualities already mentioned, the non-Christians of Carolan are also excellent workers. They produce rice, corn, tobacco, and all kinds of tubers such as yams (*ubi*)[124] and taro (*gabi*).[125] They have traded with the coastal towns near Carolan since antiquity, bartering, buying and selling. No one has or has had the slightest fear or apprehension about going to their territory, sleeping or trading among them. There has not been any unfortunate insult, robbery, or aggression on the part of the non-Christians. They do not permit evil doers to seek refuge among them or harbor fugitives from the Christian towns.

The fierceness, recklessness, and hospitality of the Carolanians has been attested by an event which occurred thirty-eight years ago. In 1856 two Recollect priests started preparing the Carolanians for conversion to the Christian faith. Fortunately, the two priests are still alive. One is in Minuluan--young in thought, still active and enterprising at a relatively advanced age. The

---

[124]*Ubi* or *Discorea alata* ". . .is the most important of all the yams and is usually the yam referred to by writers when they simply mention yam" (Brown 1957 1:386).

[125]*Gabi* is taro (Brown 1957 1:348).

other priest lives in Spain, still an impetuous and determined man but without life or light in his eyes. For the purpose of an immediate *reducción*, they were given a special commission by the governor of the Island, Don Emilio Saravia.

They entered into pacts and agreements which the non-Christians generally accepted but asked first for time to harvest their rich and abundant crops. Once the harvest had been gathered, they would begin the *reducción*, building houses in those places that the authorities designated as the best and most healthful.

This was what the Carolanian non-Christians agreed to do. The priests were given gifts. They spent the night among the non-Christians, well attended and respected. As a sign of the seriousness of their commitment, a group of thirty of the most important members of the non-Christians accompanied the priests to Kabankalan. There they met with the governor who accepted their offers and agreed to the time they sought in the name of their chief, Manyabog. The governor received them affectionately and paternally, giving them gifts and various presents which they valued. Thus was the contract made, agreeing to the terms established by the two priests with Manyabog.

This fruitful work, leading to such Christian and patriotic ends, was detrimental to people engaged in trade and business with the non-Christians, taking from them their authority and profits.[126] As on some occasions, the evil arts conquered. The Machiavellianism of a few people (now gone from the region) came to rest in the governor, gaining force in his vehemence of character and temperament as well as taking advantage of the ignorance and simplicity of the non-Christians.

From that moment on, reneging on everything promised Manyagog by the priests and himself, the governor hastened the *reducción*. He believed that arms could do that which patience, constancy, and peaceful methods could have achieved in a few years.

Determined in the idea suggested by those persons who, with the passage of time, must be named, the governor prepared to enter Carolan with a force of 450 civilian police (*comisarios*), armed with bolos, and sixty men from a division of the *Guardia Civil* (*Tercios de Policía*) armed with rifles, two cannons (*cañones*), and ammunition. This squad was led to the mountains under the command of a sergeant-of-police, a Spaniard named Don Pedro Matanzas.

---

[126]According to Varona "In today's language, they could be referred to as a rich and tempting market for underhanded exploiters who knew it would serve their evil purposes to have Manyabog and his immense tribe remain outside the margins of law and order" (1938:4th Installment).

When the force arrived at a place called Lapjan, in the center of Carolan, all the non-Christians had been warned by those who had set the trap for the governor and the non-Christians. Matanzas found a large number of hostile people, most of them in a *cotta*, a kind of fort made of trees. The vicinity of the *cotta* was protected by more Carolanians who had taken positions at high and strategic points. And then a strange thing happened. Without warning, without an attempt at conciliation, without hinting at the surrender of the people who days before had presented themselves humble and obedient, without consideration of the efforts made by the two religious men in arriving at a pact and their promises, the guns were fired.

They opened fire with shots and cannon, while the non-Christians refrained from full battle, hoping that the fighting would turn to man-to-man combat. While Manyabog lived, in spite of the deaths caused by the guns, the non-Christians defended themselves. When a bullet killed Manyabog, the non-Christians retreated to three large *cogon* thatched houses inside the fortress. They did not surrender or give up. There they carried out an act of valor and manliness which demonstrated their energy and fierceness by setting fire to the houses they were in. Many of them died of burns and asphyxiation but not without defending themselves. A lieutenant of the rural guards (*Cuadrilleros*) of Valladolid tried to enter the fort but was killed by a spear thrown from one of the windows of the houses. The result of this expedition was the death of two soldiers and four civilian police, more than eighty wounded, and many non-Christians asphyxiated in the houses.

Time has the duty of erasing the horrible impressions of this event that were so sad and harmful to the interest of the country and religion. Little by little calm and knowledge of the motives and causes that were ignored in those moments of unrest and anxiety have returned. Few memories remain. The non-Christians will forget because they are very susceptible to *reducción* if peaceful methods and the policy of smooth and compliant attraction ingrained in our system of colonization are used.

In this system the missionary is identified with the Cross, the only flag, the symbol of universal redemption. It is like a tree under whose branches all peoples may come for protection. In this system the sword is to be used only when the circumstances demand. In this system the plow and work are the bonds of unity which today, for the glory of both governed and governing, brings unity in brotherhood to the inhabitants of the island of Negros.

CHAPTER XIII

A TRIP IS ARRANGED

It is agreed, and it is a rare thing in the Philippines, that punctuality distinguishes visitors.

The flavored chocolate called *soconusco*[127] comes in two different qualities, sometimes called *á* or *é*, but it is delicious no matter what its quality. They say that in some houses the calm Filipino indicates which class of chocolate to serve by asking the servant to make *chocolatá* or *chocolaté*, the best to the lesser quality. There were also biscuits and cheese on the table and a water clearer than the Moncayo river gives its favored town.

It was five in the morning and the day began to clear. Violet color flooded the heavenly roof in the east, and it was still possible to see some stars. In the western sky the moon was disappearing behind white opalescent clouds. The mountains begin to appear clearly and a light breeze moves the bamboo and the palms sway at its touch as do the tips of the sugar cane. Daylight intends to overcome the darkness of the night. The noises that precede the daily work are heard.

There is a house surrounded by a garden in which there are Spanish roses, *sampaguitas dobles*,[128] jasmine, and tube roses (*nardos*) perfuming the air. By the house door wait two athletic looking Filipinos with shotguns and wearing cartridge belts. Three saddled horses stand nearby. The horses neigh and the travelers mount them. While the bells of the hacienda and the whistle of the steam engine call the laborers, the horsemen follow a long, broad street that leads to the swamp [*mangle*, actually the mangrove tree]. The nimble servants walk behind.

---

[127] *Soconusco*, a chocolate mixed with ground vanilla and other spices, may be named for the Socunusco region of Chiapas, Mexico, famed for both its cacao and vanilla.

[128] A fragrant and popular flower of the jasmine family (*Jasminum sambac* Linn. Ait.) that often is used by Filipinos to make garlands (Brown 1957 3:221-22).

The tip of a boat mast rises above the tops of the trees, letting one discover the interior of the swamp. To the unknowing it is a surprise that among the many *pagatpat* and *bacjao*[129] trees there could be a boat, a short road, a clearing opened by felling trees with an ax, embankments, and a river. Doubt gives away to reality at the sight of a boat where four oarsmen and a man at the rudder wait. It is a small cabin boat that holds in its large bellied hull sacks of sugar unloaded from the cars of the tramway. The tide rises, growing every moment; the pink shrimp scurry and hide at a noise. The nets taken from the water are filled with abundant small fish.

"Let's go!" shouts the owner of the boat as the three waiting travelers take their seats. Forward, march, to the steady beat and force of the four oars. The boat stops, aground. The oarsmen and owner jump into the water. On command, they make ready, and on hearing the loud and energetic voice of the owner "At three," they push hard and the little boat returns to the channel. There it begins its zigzag progress anew, turning and maneuvering until it comes to the place where the alligator has its lair.

In the distance the whistle of a steam launch and the cooing of a dove can be heard. A tree which seeks to grow in a sandbar in the middle of the river is the only one which thrives surrounded by salt water. The tree is saluted for it adds beauty to the trip and the scene.

The flags and streamers of a steam launch fill the air. The boat that moves over the water with the help of oars pauses a moment, recognizing the superiority of that which goes by steam power. Handkerchiefs are waved, greetings are exchanged, and the passengers are transferred. The sea is calm like a lake. The *lorchas*, those boats of slender shape which carry within their thin planks the fortune of a planter or the savings of some businessman, pass by on their own routes. Coincidentally going in the same direction as the steam launch is a two-masted vessel (*vilox*) that points its prow toward a solid and unmoving bulk which appears in the sea about two miles from the beach.

A canvas awning can be seen in the distance. Now the *palma bravas* can be seen growing in the sand. The eyes of a hundred people are fixed on the little steamer which speeds up to reach the end of its trip. They begin to count the small boats that surround the fish corral (*ponot*). [A fish corral is a large, often semicircular, offshore bamboo fish trap.][130] The corral is none other than the destination of these travelers.

---

[129]See footnote 113.

[130]For additional information on the fish corrals of southern Negros Oriental, see Hart 1956.

The corral is built in water about fourteen meters deep. It represents unending work, constancy, and fast decision. It requires an exceptional diver with lungs that can withstand the deep water. To build a corral one must combine bamboo, rattan, and *palma brava* and take into account the desirability of the site, currents, tides, and winds.

The natural aptitude of the Filipino worker, this quality of genius that is part of his constitution, towers in this handiwork in the middle of the sea. For several months were combined intelligence and industry, business and profit, the investor and the worker, the owner of six hundred or seven hundred pesos, and a person with lungs forged from steel and a treasure hidden in his muscles and heart.

It is an easy step from the launch to what the diver (and he who is not a diver) calls the *hormâ del corral*.[131] On the *hormâ* is found a table with bottles of Jerez, red wine (*tinto*) and Jules Robin cognac. At one side are a *calan*[132] [under which a fire] begins to burn, curtains that protect against the indiscreet glance, a rattan basket (*batulang*), a frying pan, bottles of cooking fat, cooked rice (*kanoñ*),[133] and thirty or forty people.

The divers, who wear on their bare bodies only a narrow loin cloth (*bajaque* or *bahâg*),[134] prepare the small fish net (*sijod*),[135] and throw it into the water. Others gather the fish net while the divers swim past and scrape at the *palma bravas* which form the upright posts of the corral. They disturb the fish, harrass and chase them into a reduced circle where they must be caught.

Now the case is tried. The impatience of the invited guests and the desire of the curious to discover the fortune or misfortune, knowledge or stupidity of the builders, cannot be contained. The builder's curiosity has been satisfied already because it is an established custom for the fishermen of the Island to visit the corral the day before, and to make an attempt which, if it comes out well, is not used. Instead they throw back [the fish] into the sea [within the corral] that which luck has given to them.

---

[131]Refers to the central portion of the trap, not to the fence leading to its entrance.

[132]*Calan* or *kalân* is an iron tripod on which cooking pots are placed (Kaufmann n.d.:378).

[133]*Kanoñ* is food, especially cooked rice (Kaufmann n.d.:393).

[134]See Kaufmann n.d.:75.

[135]See Kaufmann n.d.:836.

The strongest, most experienced diver seizes the small fish net which is to raise the fish from below. A long rope tied to the net is prepared beforehand which will help with the weight that can increase if the catch is a lucky one. The diver with this device disappears into the water, within the circle of the [larger] fish net (*siguin*). The fish, noticing that a strange body has come among them, become restless, rise, dive, appear on the surface of the water, and descend imprisoned by chains of narrow bamboo. [This is a reference to the underwater posts of the corral that are surrounded with a tightly woven rattan mesh that keeps the fish inside the trap]. A minute and a half passes, and at an agreed upon signal, he who is eight *brazas* below the water advises those above, who gather and haul rope, and more rope, until the strong, close net appears out of the water. The slashing tails of the mackerel (*tanguingui*)[136] are stronger than those of the barracuda (*rompecandados*).[137] The *lison*[138] strains and flaps its fins against the *bâdlon*.[139] The *ampahan*[140] wants to regain its liberty. This great variety of fish is of scarce and rare types, tasty and delicious to eat. The water flies from the splashing of the tails of the imprisoned fish who in leaping lose body scales which fly in the faces and onto the clothes of those who watch such lively work.

Cries of satisfaction escape from various sides. The owner smiles and the divers talk and recall similar cases. The buyers are quiet, thinking of the lower prices that will result from such an abudance of fish. Only the tourists and guests think of the nourishment that will result from this great variety of fish in mayonnaise sauce, *au gratin*, fried, with rice, and a thousand other kinds of cooking, sauces and seasonings.

The first excursion to the bottom [of the sea in the corral] was profitable. The buyers offer a large sum of money for fish that fit into a big basket. But the following day is Good Friday and the owner refuses. The haggling begins; the spectators become impatient. All--buyers, divers, owner, and witnessess--are animated by the thought of a new excursion of greater profit than the first.

---

[136] *Tanigi* or *tangigi* is *Scomberomorus commerson* (Herre and Umali 1948:58).

[137] *Rompecandados* (Sp. lock-breakers) or *rumpe* are large barracuda, *Sphyraena jello* (Herre and Umali 1948:46).

[138] *Lison* are either Family *Carangidae* or *tamban lison* or oil sardine, *Sardinella longiceps* (Herre and Umali 1948:52, 54).

[139] *Bâdlon* is *Gnathanodon speciosus* (Herre and Umali 1948:51).

[140] *Ampahan* or *ampajan* (spelled both ways by Echaúz) is Family *Carangidae* (Herre and Umali 1948:54).

From Iloilo and Jaro came the bargainers who are attracted by the quality and good taste of the fish and by the profit which should be great. The bidding begins again; the retail sale is started. Those who care to buy on a large scale bid to defend themselves. The auction in the middle of the sea has begun.

The steamer *Rapido* comes into sight. Fried fish, flattened and dusted lightly with flour and beaten egg, and fish cooked with fragrant herbs to be garnished later with a vinagrette sauce are brought to the table.

The owner fills his empty travel bag with Mexican pesos. The fish, strung after closing the deal, go from the corral to the boats in strings prepared as they will be eaten by the happy inhabitants of Iloilo who enjoy the prodigality and wealth of the island of Negros.

It was Good Friday and Good Friday means that steamers and *lorchas* will leave on the sandy beach and in the storerooms boxes and more boxes of hats, shoes, pieces of silk (*canton*), black wool, coconut fiber for mats, silk skirts, fans, and thousands of items that the Chinese, those Philippine ants, carefully have brought from their headquarters in Iloilo.

The haciendas are full of workers; never in those 365 days of the year, according to the roll book, have more workers come. The grower is content. The storehouse of rice vomits *gantas* and *cavanes*, and all the tasks are done with amazing promptness. At two in the morning *arronzadores*,[141] *panseadores*, *azucareros*, *soplillos* (firemen), and all the riff-raff that carries the heaviest load of the hacienda, have filled their positions; not one is missing. They have not failed one second in their respective jobs which last at least some twenty hours to make up for the delays of the coming week.

The day is beautiful, shiningly bright and clear. The sun's rays fall straight down on the sweating backs of the workers who without sitting for a moment plant sugar cane points for four hours. The northeast breeze begins to blow. The tides rise, and taking advantage of the abundant water, the boat arrives and casts anchor at the dock of the hacienda. It carries rattan, sacks, and plenty of money which will bring joy to the worker anxious to buy things for the first time. It brings satisfaction to the Chinese who in his avaricious aims is not content with less than thirty percent profit. It also brings sadness to the hacienda owner who, after religiously paying the workers, perhaps will see at the sound of the work bell on Easter Monday that many of his workers have disappeared.

---

[141]Men who pushed the cane on the feeding tables of the mill to within reach of the *panseadores*.

An interminable procession comes to the hacienda house. In the space (*silong*) below the raised floor of the house, the manager has paper in hand, the scribe is noting, and the foreman is reading names in a loud voice. They have no time to rest, not even a moment or even worse if the turn belongs to a woman who, always disposed to talk, loses nothing in the occupation of asking.

One by one they continue to appear, self-possessed, with the "I want what's coming to me" of the workers when they deal with money. At the pay table, organization, proper behavior, shame, constancy, and the value of their work disappear as each worker tries to get his share. The lazy and worthless one, who always looks for a good day, or the kind of work which best suits his lazy, loafing constitution, or comes to the roll call goaded by hunger and necessity, asks for the same reward as one who for a whole year has carried the work load nearly all of the time, bearing the rains, wind, sun, and [the task of filling] the warehouse. The *narra* [a fine Philippine wood] table contains piles of pesos which would astonish him who furnishes the expenses of the hacienda. The workers come near and ask "eight, ten, twelve pesos" that are given without hesitation to those who have earned them. A mocking smile rises to the lips of the hacienda owner when one of the lazy workers who with shameless effrontery and unequalled cynicism, on being asked how much he wants, answers "twelve." He had worked, according to the roll, only fourteen days the last two months--precisely those just before payday.

Full of money and eager to spend it, the women go hastily to the town, running here and there, to buy hats, shoes, trousers, skirts, and shirts, an anisette called *tanduay* (rum) and *tûba*. In a field of cane near the house, and in the roads where the eyes of the owner do not reach, the remainder of the money given in the morning passes through the final stage of its possession in the hands of the worker.

A poor and dim oil light, guarded from the wind to prevent a fire, is to be found in the glass of a lantern. It lights a field of cane, and a group of some forty men are reflected in its first pale light. There is a worker, a cook by trade, of thin body, penetrating looks, and large hands, the left one which holds dirty cards clasped with the eagerness that marks his whole posture. In his right hand he has a cigar full of ash and *amaraduras* known as *piokôs*.[142] "*Taya*" (Bet) he says in a low voice, turning the first cards. [The game is monte]. After the bets are made, he exclaims "*Vira*" (*Birá*, Open) and turns the card and throws it onto a pinkish cloth spread for that purpose. It is the first card of the pile of discards. All in that moment have but a single thought--to win, to win.

---

[142] *Piokôs* is "A cigar rolled for private use at home. . ." (Kaufmann n.d.:756).

The guards of the hacienda have left their posts on learning of the game. A pair from the *Guardia Civil*, noting their absence, goes to find them. While under a small house they hear talk and discussion of the game. The guards go upstairs and force the inhabitants to show them the place where the game is being held.

Cautiously, step by step, they near the place of the game, hear some words and see moving figures. They fall on them and shout, "Stop, Stop!" The lantern disappears, the cards fly, the money escapes--two *pesetas*, four cards, and two players are the body of the crime, the means of conviction, and proof of the game. The guards run, but the players, more experienced, hide in the cane fields, rivers, and bottom lands. The alarm bell rings, sounded by the guards, and with a boldness unequaled--some clean and fresh, others dirty with clay and limping--they run to tell the proprietor what has happened.

On the following day, the new hats have gone to better hands, the shoes have changed owners, and the pants have been sold for less than they cost. The lovers of luxury of Holy Week wrap themselves in the same clothes they wore months before.

Saturday [the group] continued the trip, arriving Sunday in the town of --------[omitted in original], famed for its cocks and cockfighting. And that was the way it happened.

Enter thou the temple of the fighting cock. Pass thou through a bamboo door at whose edges, on portable tables or on the floor, thou findest *paccio*,[143] boiled rice, fried fish, pickled fish, salted pressed fish (*binuro*), tidbits, and *tûba* in abundance. Cross thou a broad space, shielded from the sun by a cover of woven nipa where boast those roosters of varied colors, of showy feathers. There are the red (*pulâ*), *camasojon* [a rooster with black and white feathers], *tabâs* [a rooster with red and white feathers], and *alimbuyog* [a rooster with more black than red feathers]--all arrogant in their bindings. According to the whim of the god Success, they will be fortified through enthusiasm, applauded, celebrated, reviled, and mocked.

You pay if you are a person of little importance. They give you a ticket or paper which gives you the right to enjoy the circus from the kitchen of the organizer's assistant or the subleasor of the cockfight. You open a door of *barasbaras*[144] where a guard will, according to your appearance, either greet or only push you inside. You walk a short distance among the cane clear

---

[143]*Paccio* probably is *pako* (*Athyrium esculentum* Copel), a widespread fern whose young fronds are eaten cooked or raw. It is sold in the markets (Brown 1957 1:44-45).

[144]*Barasbaras* refers to the door made of small (1-2 inches in diameter) sticks of mangrove wood.

of weeds. You are now in the track, on the soil, in this ring where classes do not exist. Here the Spaniard, the past *capitán*, *teniente*, *gobernadorcillo*, *comisarios*, laborer, and the head of the village (*barangay*) become equal.

This is the place where the aspirations of all are one, where impressions are confused, shouts rise spontaneously, and boasts fix values. Here money, whether the son of toil or the product of some irregularity, passes from hand to hand like a sack of puppets. All are the same in this ring in which you can read in big letters the apotheosis of the vice, explaining as it does in a sign of regular dimensions: *Box Seats for Spaniards* and *Professional Gamblers Preferred.*

Turn your head and observe three groups of from twelve to fourteen individuals, all squatting who touch, feel, and handle the cocks which are on the large veranda (*palayas*)[145] inside the arena. In a place very near the fighting ring, people come and go, draw near and retreat. Servants, friends, or relatives carry the roosters back and forth. They are placed in the middle of the group of people, for what is called the *emparejar* (the pairing of the cocks), who examine the size, length, form, and weight of those who are to fight. The pairing requires great care and attention, fine appreciation and knowledge on the part of a skillful participant. These qualities come from the inborn temperament of the individual who looks and observes the cock's guts (*tenaza*), scales, scars, body, ears, eyes, and beak.

After speaking with others, praising and extolling the strange biped, and underrating one's own with praise and insults, sayings and jokes, the roosters are paired. Low-voiced gossiping groups form and flow as an ebb tide toward the previously abandoned cock pit. They grow and reach their greatest animation if the match is between two cocks of powerful and wealthy owners based on some earlier fight, between cocks from different islands or opposing towns who are rivals in their fiestas or economic progress.

A *navajero* [one who fixes the blade to the cock's spur] or the owner takes out the blades, examines, measures, and sharpens them. He finally selects one which he hones on the stone. He takes the blade in his teeth, with the point toward his nose and its eye down, beginning in this instant the most important act, one of the greatest consequence for the game of the cocks.

A trusted servant, perhaps he who with attention and solicitude cared for the cock for months by exercising, bathing, massaging, and putting vinegar on its legs and head and smoking its wings

---

[145]An addition to the house as a balcony, annex, or veranda (Kaufmann n.d.:622). In the Glossary this word as defined is meaningless.

with the strongest tobacco to kill bugs [lice or mites], takes the cock in his left arm. He holds it with the beak toward his heart as if he wished to bestow upon it some enduring caress, to give of his courage and enthusiasm to the cock who will soon need it in the fight.

The *navajero* seizes the left leg, the one with the trimmed and tended spur, and extends it to the binder. He massages and pets the rooster very slowly as the sheepskin or paper on which the blade is to be attached is put over the spur. The blade is adjusted over the spur and fixed. He takes a step back without letting go of the leg. He looks from the tip of the blade to the other end, examines and compares it. He is lost in a thousand calculations of the advantages of straight or curved blades. He puts the blade on, if it is to his liking, giving a hundred turns of cord, fine silk, or twisted thread. Then the sheath is put over the blade's edge. The claws of the bird are stretched to regain elasticity and agility, if that ability has been lost by binding the leg with so much thread.

The cocks are put in the cock pit. The night before they had been visited at twelve or one in the morning by their respective owners in the tenuous and dim light of a candle or a glass of oil shielded by a tissue paper shade. Those cocks, who had been found sleeping or resting in a position like a snake, or looking at their bindings, or seeming like sharks (*baguis*), are about to fight. For them the tides, moon, Sagittarius, Pisces, Capricorn, feathers, and their color have been consulted. There are those who have their claws curled like a corkscrew (*tira-buson*) or whose legs beat like a drum roll (*dao dedoble sa tambor*). And there are those whose scars on their spurs are painted black or who have a beak and wings that brings them credit.

Piles and piles of pesos appear on the table of the house. It matters little that there is a rule about limiting the size of the bets. In this matter, all classes meet, inquiring and asking: Listen! It lacks a little. That's over. Pay! Take it out! I add one or two!--meaning one or two hundred pesos. The table is too small for so much money and so many people. The players go from one side to the other, forgetting their traditional laziness. The confusion is frightening, bets are made crossing from here to there. From corner to corner questions are asked--running, animating conversations. Tales are told of the cocks, of their pedigrees, play, life, miracles, the fights they have won, and their manner of fighting.

The noisy confusion and uproar are mixed with smiles and happy remarks. There is a smell of tobacco--an odor, an animation and air of enthusiasm in the gaming house that excites and enervates a public eager to win or lose, for the most part, and looking for impressions from the most unlikely source. Everyone is agitated in this intoxicating atmosphere borne only by the true fan. This air is breathable only by the owners of the cocks who are excited in contemplating the idol of the house, by him who desires a just cockfight, and by he who has pride, vanity, confidence, and knowledge of the rooster.

The voice of the manager crying "*Pica y larga*"--"Let them bite and turn them loose"--reaches the ears of those who are in the cock pit (*gallera*). A bell rings to announce that all bets are made and covered. The arena is cleared of people. They are pushed out of the way for there is no other way to move them in this place crazed by money and the cocks. Only the handlers, judges, and the spokesman remain in the arena. The owners or handlers grasp the cock known as the *llamado*, the betting favorite. He is held in the left arm, with his head covered by the right hand, leaving only the ears uncovered to be pecked at by the *dejado*, the less favored cock. The *dejado* pecks with fury. Then the operation is reversed, with the favorite pecking the *dejado*.

Now the sheath is removed; the steel knife is brilliant and shining. The judge and spokesman move to one side, from this moment on to observe attentively and in detail both the handlers and the cocks. Now the crucial questions begin--what of the lines, inpsiration and favored terrain? In these matters, the handlers show great skill and knowledge because any carelessness or disadvantage could be fatal.

All is silence in the cock pit. Not a single sound is heard. Nobody speaks. All are mute; sight replaces tongues. No movement of the handlers is overlooked that might be disputed. Taking advantage of the superstitions innate to the players of blood, not a single location of the bird, or the direction of the sun, not a slight uneveness of the ground, overlooked in the assistant's preparations, escapes their attention. They watch for carelessness, laxity, or the slightest indiscretion.

Finally, after changes from one side to the other, comparisons, turns, a thousand triangulations and plottings, the cocks are put on the ground at a distance calculated by their disposition to be quick or slow to attack, or to fly a lot, or to fight above or below. There are a thousand other reasons reserved to the profane who do not find the cause of their ignorance, who seek neither diversion in the events, who look not to the ability of the cock with the knife, but blame it all on luck as if it were not the unappealable arbiter of all games and the value of cocks did not vary from four *reales* to fifty or sixty pesos.

The cocks are now face to face. They lower their tails which before were as high as their combs. A circle of small feathers rises on their long necks. The beak is low, going from side to side as it tries to distract its opponent. Eyes are fixed on the movements of the combatant. Both fear attack. They dig their open claws into the ground, shake their small heads--a sure sign of a good fighting cock. They protect their breasts as if they knew the seriousness of a wound there. The cocks fly with broad wings extended. The steel, by a single contraction of the claws, comes to be both defense and offense, the protection of one and the cause of injury to the other. The two fight well; they are accomplished fencers. They have not butted at each other. They return to the ground. Their courage is worth more than all the tactics and fencing taught those Mondays in the *sampoc* [sessions where cocks are taught to fight].[146]

They attack angrily; the second time they hit with zeal. Blow after blow is struck. One falls, trying to defend itself. It almost dies. Or both, badly wounded, flee because of the pain. The sentence is passed. The winning cock is given to one of the handlers to receive the caresses, praise, and company due the victor. The loser, like all losers, goes to loneliness, insult, and calumny. But it is not always like this. Cocks have been known to return, after losing, through some unexplainable circumstance, and having been cured of their wounds, to win with courage.

---

[146]See Glossary.

CHAPTER XIV

THE PARISH MISSIONS (*MISIONES PARRAQUIAS*) AND THE FRONTIER MISSIONS (*MISIONES VIVAS*)

The authorities, *poblacion* officials, and persons living both in and out of Negros are concerned with reason about the type of life, unsettling risks, and burdens carried and suffered by the farmers and workers today engaged in the clearing and cultivation of the forests and fields of the Island.

Those most directly interested in finding a remedy for these problems could not help trying to find a solution. In 1856 the Governor of the Province, Don Emilio Saravia, sent a statement to His Excellency, the Governor-General [of the Philippines]. This statement was accompanied by a report and a general census based on data collected by the Recollect Fathers from barrio to barrio and sitio to sitio. The priests were motivated by nothing more than a desire to incorporate into the social life of the Island all those they found outside of it. They designated that missions should be established at Batoc (today Zaragoza), Manpunay, Buñgajin Calactcat, and Carolan. It is not known whether these suggestions were carried out.

Later the Most Reverend Father Pedro Sanz of Jimamaylan, who is well-remembered, published a pamphlet about the missions, full of data and information. These facts were of use to an illustrious Governor, His Excellency Don Valeriano Weyler[147] in bringing his never well-liked projects for *repartimiento de enlace*[148] which included in its organization of the province an appropriate adjustment for the particular conditions of the Island whose major agricultural development was moving towards the mountains.

At that time, under the administration of that same illustrious Governor-General, a project for missions and a brief review

[147]Valeriano Weyler was Governor-General of the Philippines from 1888 to 1891.

[148]*Repartimiento de enlace* appears to refer to the custom of forcing Filipinos to work a certain number of days each year on public works.

of the island of Negros was published. The author, the Most Reverend Father Mauricio Ferrero, vicar of the southern part of the western region, dedicated his work to the Marquis of Tenerife [the largest of the Canary Islands]. Some of the ideas in this publication have found more complete realization than could have been expected.

The Governor-General was not an authority given to forgetting ideas received in a flattering way. In one of his first visits to the provinces he came unannounced to Negros where he saw, inspected, and encouraged the Recollect priests to continue their efforts. He ordered his aides to help establish boundaries and lines of demarcation. Today, although an important power in Spain and far from the Philippines, he is still remembered for his interesting and necessary projects.

The negotiations did not stop. By the end of 1893, the Most Reverend Provincial of the Recollects, Father Mariano Bernad, turned to the Governor-General for help in a petition, as reasoned as it was practical, for the establishment of the parish missions and active or frontier missions on the Island. These missions were to solve the problems for both country and religion.

The highest authorities of the islands always supported those ideas which had useful and successful ends. Because they wished to bring welfare and prosperity to those who needed it, they quickly and willingly agreed to turn over the customary information from the western region. This was to be expected, considering the antecedents of the present governor. The Illustrious Bishop of the Diocese, in his turn, sent a canonical order to the vicars, informing them of the merit of this far-reaching task. Also included in the order were numerical data, detailed information, and general knowledge of the province which had been gained from previous studies and through the courage of Father Patricio Adell and Father Mauricio Ferrero.

One must travel from the year 1849, the date of the re-incorporation of the island of Negros under the Recollect priests, to the present to observe with scrupulous attention the policies followed on all occasions--with the exception of the unfortunate Carolanian campaign which was interrupted by shortsightedness and greed--to form accurate ideas with respect to colonization and a practical means of progressing without delay or difficulty.

We have seen the priest, Spaniard, and Filipino united, favored at the same time by the activities and energies of the governing authorities. It has been possible to admire the good working qualities of the Filipino, solely and alone, as he leaves trade for agriculture, in the clearing of lands, the opening of roads, and the establishment and laying out of haciendas. The Filipino has valued and followed the footsteps of the Spaniard, building drainage ditches, improving farming techniques, and in other matrial improvements. The Filipino and the Spaniard have learned to build water-powered and abaca decortification machines under the guidance and generosity of the Recollects.

Thus we witness the catechism, the agricultural work, and the idea of country, represented in the priest, the Spaniard, the Filipino, and authority, as long as they stay together, continue in prosperity, defending, teaching, and working, all for one, stimulated by the commonweal and the exaltation of their common Mother.

The Filipino worker with the ax goes before all, suffering the tyranny of sickness, bad food, little sleep, clearing trees, burning bushes, planting root crops, rice, and corn. He is followed by the Filipino proprietor and the Spaniard setting out haciendas, building houses, carrying on the cultivation of sugar, abaca, and coffee, protected by the priest who sends them a companion to visit (if he is alone in the church) to encourage and fortify them. He makes them [Spaniards and proprietors] worthy of consideration in the eyes of the workers, praying and counseling. He teaches the wise lessons of the Gospel--love and respect for the authorities and for their subordinates.

The priest cannot do everything he wants. The distance that separates his church from the barrio or sitio, which is the object of his labors, is twenty or twenty-five kilometers of roads that are mudholes, that are chasms so deep not even carabaos can pass. For this reason, neither the action of the government nor the help of the church reaches these places.

The frontier and parish missions will respond to a civilizing principle, Christian and patriotic, and to administrative and economic goals which will result in an enthusiastic blossoming of the sentiments of the Spaniard, the Catholic, the governors, and the economists. It [the principle] will assist in developing the protection and defense due the inhabitants of the forest who contribute their proportional share to the duties of the state and yet do not receive any benefits. Assistance must be given those who belong to the community of the faithful who, powerless to act, do not want thousands of persons, without restraints or controls, to live in a savage manner without being of benefit to anyone other than their own absurd beliefs and inveterate errors.

The island of Negros, worked and working on the shore, has moved, in its population growth and desire for progress, toward the mountains. Each assumed step of the advance of civilization to the interior is a force that hides the problems of certain people. These are the *sacadas* and the non-Christians for whose *reducción* and attraction the proposed missions were to be established.

The missions will be comprised of the following:

PARISH MISSIONS WITH $600

Southern Vicariate of the Western Region:

Suay with Binicuil of Jimamaylan.
San Miguel with the Carlota farm.

Frontier Missions with 800 Pesos and 400 Pesos for the Assistant:

Alegría with Sta. Rosa of Murcia.
Cumalisquis of Murcia.
Odiong of La Isabela.
Carolan of Kabankalan.
Campomanes of Sipalay.

Western Vicariate of the North:

San Cárlos with Guadalupe and Jagna of Calatrava.
Argüelles with Magallanes and Marianas of Escalante.
Sicaba with Cádiz Viejo and Chamberí of Cádiz Nuevo.
Victorias of Manapla.
Kabankalan of Saravia.

Frontier Missions with 800 Pesos and 400 Pesos for the Assistant:

Eastern Vicariate of the North:

Bagabuinis with Tabon and Gilaitan of Guiljuñgan.
Toboso and Salamanca of Escalante.
Honot-honot of Escalante.

Detailed figures are given for all the parish and frontier missions to aid in understanding them. Let us begin with the northern part of the western region and end with the southern part of the same region.[149]

Parish Missions

1ST CALATRAVA

Jurisdiction of the Mission	Distance from the Main Mission	Number of Christians	*Sacadas*	Non-Christians
San Cárlos	27 kilometers	3,000		
Guadalupe	30 "	1,800	2,000	4,000
Jagna	33 "	1,200		

[149]Echaúz used >> which has been translated as ditto when placed under kilometers and zero when used in the columns for *sacadas* and non-Christians.

The soil, of first class quality, produces 24,000 *picos* of sugar, tobacco, cacao, rice, and some abaca.

2ND ESCALANTE

Jurisdiction of the Mission	Distance from the Main Mission	Number of Christians	*Sacadas*	Non-Christians
Argüelles Magallanes Marianas	20 kilometers 30 " 34 "	4,441 1,400 1,600	2,500	1,000

Excellent land on which 40,000 *picos* of sugar are harvested including abundant amounts of corn and root crops.

3RD CÁDIZ NUEVO

Jurisdiction of the Mission	Distance from the Main Mission	Number of Christians	*Sacadas*	Non-Christians
Sicaba Cádiz Viejo Chamberí	10 kilometers 15 " 18 "	10,000 1,250 927	7,000	0

Large portions of land from the beach to Macauili mountain are still uncultivated. There is a large and navigable river. The harvests have amounted to some 8,000 *picos* of sugar, with abundant rice, fish, and some abaca and coffee. In this mission there is enough excellent lumber, rattan, and firewood from the swamps for all the needs of agriculture.

4TH SARAVIA

Jurisdiction of the Mission	Distance from the Main Mission	Number of Christians	*Sacadas*	Non-Christians
Kabankalan	10 kilometers	3,875	8,000	0

This mission furnishes indisputable proof of the value of the *sacadas*. It is impossible for 3,875 individuals of all ages to produce more than 100,000 *picos* of sugar (which is what these fertile lands yield) let alone clear and till the land, producing as in no other part of the Island.

5TH MANAPLA

Jurisdiction of the Mission	Distance from the Main Mission	Number of Christians	*Sacadas*	Non-Christians
Victorias	12 kilometers	5,600	6,000	0

Manapla is like Saravia in regard to the value of the *sacadas*. It does not seem possible that 5,600 workers can produce more than 90,000 *picos* of sugar, plant rice, corn and root crops, fish, and tend the *cainguin* (*kaiñgin*).[150]

6TH LA CARLOTA

Jurisdiction of the Mission	Distance from the Main Mission	Number of Christians	*Sacadas*	Non-Christians
San Miguel with Model Farm	16 kilometers	10,000	6,000	3,500

The sugar output of the extensive lands that belong to this mission exceeds 80,000 *picos*. The cultivated lands have reached the lower slopes of Canlaon mountain.

7TH JIMAMAYLAN

Jurisdiction of the Mission	Distance from the Main Mission	Number of Christians	*Sacadas*	Non-Christians
Suay	6 kilometers	6,000	0	3,000

This town has a *capitán municipal* and a justice of peace. It is separated from the main mission by three rivers that make communications and help impossible when needed. It produces abundant sugar and rice.

---

[150] *Kaiñgin* is the plot (swidden) or the practice of shifting (swidden) agriculture.

Frontier Missions

1ST GUILJUÑGAN

Jurisdiction	Distance	Number of Christians	Non-Christians
Baganinis Tabon Jilaitan	30 kilometers 36 " 40 "	500	9,500

In this mission, fixed in its territory, is the nearest narrow valley for communication between both the eastern and western regions. At the foot of the beautiful valley, in the eastern part, Don Diego de la Viña has established himself. He is a practical and intelligent man, a worker of constancy and self-denial, who honors the name and title of his father, the Spaniard Don Diego Viña, an enterprising and active man. This gentleman has built a road which puts the western region into communication with the eastern by the shortest and most practical route on the Island. With his humane treatment, he has known how to gain the sympathies and affection of the mountain people [*monteses*] who live on the rim of the valley. He gives protection, help, and hospitality to all transients who, in passing from one coast to the other, seek shelter in his house. He plants rice, corn, and root crops, and raises all kinds of animals.

In the entire valley and jurisdiction of this mission are produced 4,000-5,000 *cavanes* of corn, 20,000 hands [small tied bundles] of first class tobacco leaf, and 3,000 *cavanes* of rice. They raise rattan and *sig-id*.[151] In the abundant and fertile pastures are horses, carabaos, and cattle. The soil is suitable for all kinds of cultivation and the area has drinking water and flowing rivers.

2ND ESCALANTE

Jurisdiction	Distance	Number of Christians	*Sacadas*	Non-Christians
Toboso Salamanca	30 kilometers 35 "	400	0	7,600

[151]*Sig-id* (*Ichnocarpus volubilis* (Lour.) Merr.) is a woody vine used for tying purposes in making fences, fish corrals, etc. (Brown 1957 3:240). In southern Negros *sig-id* is not grown but is gathered wild in the mountains.

There is excellent first class timber on the mountains. Abundant corn and tubers are harvested and the soil is excellent for tobacco, abaca, and coffee.

3RD ESCALANTE

Jurisdiction	Distance	Number of Christians	*Sacadas*	Non-Christians
Honot-honot	24 kilometers	0	0	3,000

In this area are found great veins of coal, evidence of mines where excavations, samples, and tests have been made. In general, the lands are useful for the cultivation of sugar cane. The mission will be situated near the Danao river. This is a very deep river which could be used by deep draught boats. After some years it will be the point of embarcation, the port of the island of Negros. This will occur when the material and agricultural progress of Negros has reached the height that is to be expected, given the rapid and prodigious advance of these last years.

4TH MURCIA

Jurisdiction	Distance	Number of Christians	*Sacadas*	Non-Christians
Alegría Sta. Rosa	10 kilometers 15 "	2,500	0	2,500

Here are fertile lands which grow all kinds of products: rice, corn, root crops such as camotes of various classes, *ubi*, taro, *barot*,[152] *lima-lima*,[153] *tinancong*,[154] *cambava*, abaca, *quinsol*,[155] *halbay*,[156] *moro*,[157] and *mundo*[158] [a variety of banana]. •First class coffee grows in abundance, most of it the *caraolillo* type.

---

[152]*Barot* (Ceb. *barut*) is the poorest quality of tobacco (Wolff 1972 1:116).

[153]*Lima-lima* (Bisayan: *sapang*) is a plant (*Dioscorea pentaphylla* Linn.) raised or sought in the wild state for its edible tubers (Brown 1957 1:402).

[154]According to informants a vegetable, similar to camote leaves, that may be cooked as a vegetable or fed raw to the pigs.

[155]Unidentified vegetable.

[156]Unidentified vegegable.

[157]*Moro* may be *vetiver* (*Andropogon zizanioides* (Linn. Urban) whose fragrant roots are used to weave fans (Brown 1957 1:94).

[158]See Kaufmann n.d.:594.

5TH MURCIA

Jurisdiction	Distance	Number of Christians	*Sacadas*	Non-Christians
Cumalisquis	40 kilometers	0	0	3,000

The leader of Murcia, Abnay, has sworn to recognize and to be subordinate to Spain. He did this before the civil authorities of Murcia and its parish priest, Father Miguel de las Angustias, who knows how to control him with his policies of attraction.

The valleys and ravines of this mission produce a surprising amount of coffee, abaca, cacao, and tobacco considering its very backward methods of cultivation. There are many *ilang-ilang* trees and *bitá*,[159] the quinine known among Filipinos, grows wild there. Tar, resin, rubber (*caucho*), and *gutta percha*[160] are easily extracted from wild trees.

6TH LA ISABELA

Jurisdiction	Distance	Number of Christians	*Sacadas*	Non-Christians
Odiong	20 kilometers	11,415	4,000	5,000

Located at the foot of Canlaon, La Isabela governs the towns of Pontevedra, Ginigaran, and La Isabela. Preferred crops are rice and considerable sugar cane. Its lands are first class and, according to practical tests, easily grows ramie (*ramio*) and indigo (*añil*).[161]

The lands at the present time are the object of projects and studies that, when realized, will cause an agricultural revolution in Negros. These projects deal with the establishment of a central

[159]*Bitá* (*Alstonai scholaris* (Linn. R. Br.) is a tree whose bark has medicinal uses, but it is not true quinine (Brown 1957 3:231,339-43).

[160]*Gutta percha* is the sap of the *Achras zapota* (Linn.) which is valued in the Philippines primarily for its fruit, *chico* (Brown 1957 3:190-93).

[161]Two species of indigo have been cultivated in the Philippines: *tayum* (Pan. *tágum*) or *Indigofera Suffruiticosa* (Mill.) and *tayum-tayuman* (Pan. *tágum*) or *Indigofera tinctoria* (Linn.) (Brown 1957 2:119-20). Also see Kaufmann n.d.:882.

factory (*fabrica central*), on terms acceptable to those who live from the earth, and the construction of an economical steam-powered tramway. This enterprise is being undertaken by a commercially astute and patriotic individual.

7TH KABANKALAN

Jurisdiction	Distance	Number of Christians	*Sacadas*	Non-Christians
Carolan	24 kilometers	0	0	13,000

This sitio, without a doubt, is the best of all places within the island of Negros. Its extensive jurisdiction, fertile lands, fresh and agreeable climate make it suitable for all classes of crops. Its tobacco brings double the ordinary price and its root crops are excellent. In earlier times, when hunger like a destructive plague came to be a punishment, the products of Carolan, in large part, alleviated the unfortunate situation of the needy.

This mission includes the mountain range of Tipasi that is the route which unites the two regions.

The work of the missionary will turn out to be difficult but shall be highly useful.

8TH SIPALAY

Jurisdiction	Distance	Number of Christians		Non-Christians
Campomanes	33 kilometers	500		2,500

This mission will be placed on the breast of Campomanes and on its land it will be possible to grow indigo, cotton, abaca, coffee, sugar cane, and rice.

PARTIAL RÉSUMÉ

	Number of Christians		*Sacadas*	Non-Christians	
Parish Missions:					
1st................	6,000		2,000	4,000}	
2nd................	7,441		2,500	1,000}	
3rd................	12,247	[12,177]+	7,000	0 }	
4th................	3,850	[3,875]	8,000	0 }	→ 11,500
5th................	5,600		6,000	0 }	
6th................	10,000		6,000	3,500}	
7th................	6,000		0	3,000}	
Frontier Missions:					
1st................	500		0	9,500}	
2nd................	400		0	7,600}	
3rd................	0		0	3,000}	
4th................	2,500		0	2,500}	→ 46,100
5th................	0		0	3,000}	
6th................	11,415		4,000	5,000}	
7th................	0		0	13,000}	
8th................	500		0	2,500}	
	66,453	[66,408]	35,500	57,600	

TOTAL RÉSUMÉ

Christians.............	66,453	[66,408]
Sacadas.................	35,500	
Non-Christians.........	57,600	
Total.............	159,553	[159,508]

These figures, individually and combined, are more eloquent and forceful than all the speeches that could be made in favor of establishing the missions. They save commentary and avoid all kinds of discussions.

Thousands and thousands of people are beyond the reach of all human communication. There are 57,600 humans without the slightest notion of religion or country, civilization or authority. There are also 35,500 souls far from the action of justice, escaped from their appointed village leaders, pursued by the

+Echaúz erred in transferring figures from 3rd and 4th to this table.

courts,[162] and not attending to the duties of the state. The remainder, the greatest part living without aid or protection, without guarantees or bonds of unity, force the creation of centers where, at the word of the priest and the authorities, the grouping of houses, the exhortations, and the *reducción*[163] has slowly begun. The attempt to bring families together should continue to the end. In this manner they begin to prepare the founding of towns which, in a short period of time, will be full of progress and prosperity.

And the hand of the hacienda owner, disposed as it is to move slowly in its love of economy, should not be involved in this vital work. The activities of the government which zealously guards in its mind a single point of view, *reducción* and attraction, civilization and subjugation of thousands of people, should not meddle. This problem will be settled by the growth of population which will begin to pay [the necessary expenses]. With the nucleus of the *sacadas*[164] obliged to register, they will more than pay for the expenses of the missions that will become solvent with only 10,000 *sacadas*.

Leave completely undisturbed for the moment the non-Christians who, with the passage of time, will be more individuals subject to paying taxes to the nation. The difficulty from the beginning seems resolved more than equitably. The treasury of the nation will usefully gain in all aspects. The state will add to its number of subjects. Religion will have a greater number of children. And the work in the fields will be under the protection of the authorities.

---

[162] [This footnote was added by Echaúz.] In the time [1883-1885] of His excellency, Governor-General Joaquin Jovellar [y Soler], some priests called to the attention of a Treasury Inspector (who had made a quick trip to Bacolod) the questions of the *sacadas*. This inspector made suggestions which should be found in the *Intendencia* (Office of the Chief Economic Officer).

[163] See footnote 38.

[164] See footnote 115.

CHAPTER XV

THE BABAYLANES

There is a sect which has isolated itself in the mountains. It did not originate in Negros, or live on it, for its center of propagation is not this Island. In the migration of thousands of workers, the sect has come to Negros as to all the Bisayas. It is alive in Samar, Antique [Panay], and in the mountains of Iloilo and Siaton [southern Negros Oriental].[165] It is always imitative in its purpose, always simple in its manner of uprising, and always obeys the same cause and pursues the same objective.

It is not fitting to speak in this book of the warlike *babaylanism* whose members have rifles of wood, uniforms of the *Guardia Civil*, little books of prayers to make a man invisible to bullets, and excites passions and simplicities because that would be turning away from our main objective. In this chapter *babaylanism* will be presented as a peaceful group which practices its rites in places beyond the reach of the government and the Church.

The believers of the cult are found in different islands and provinces. They believe in what appears to be their self-interest. They do not require many comforts to live. Each on his own may use some old hut in the mountains. The hut gives shade when there is sun, shelter when it rains, protection against the night, and a place to eat if one is hungry and has food. The cultist lives happily without thinking of individual rights either before or after the law. During the new moon of March, members of the cult gather in a small group. A large and solemn meeting, also in March, takes place every seven years.

As a member of a strange sect, the cultist is most zealous. He may go to town if he is pressed by need or if he is called to cure someone who is sick. He enjoys his backward state but assumes, when it suits his convenience, the regular life of a curer. In his wily instinct he combines and shares in the superior qualities of his savage life and the comforts of the civilized.

---

[165]For an account of this movement in Siaton, see Hart 1967.

He does not wear rosaries or scapularies at his neck. But in a bag, tied to his back, he carries his *anting-anting* or charm. And not believing in God, he calls to the witch, *asuwang*, or to the spirits of which he has, for his own private use, more examples, classes, and species than found in natural history. He does not raise his soul to God and does not pray. But he pleases his body, satisfies his desires, makes sacrifices, and reads his book with letters printed in various colors.

The greatest force and the strongest efforts have tried to end this superstitious sect. It is an extremely difficult task. The idea of "I" and always "I," life without work, of vice and slipperiness--the life of the three sins to which this weak nature is most prone--has made a callus, has formed a base in the *babaylan* that makes it impossible to turn him from his path so deeply rooted in the marrow of his inclinations.

A priest, Agustino Calzado, of the province of Iloilo, zealous in his duties, whose religious spirit could not tolerate such great superstitions, was treacherously and villainously killed not twenty years ago. A commander of the *Guardia Civil* energetically helped another priest who was determined that such absurd and uncivilized practices not be carried on in his parish. He managed to stop them in one place. However, the members of the sect simply moved to other places. The superstitious sect exists today. It will exist for some time to come, as long as civilization does not penetrate the sect's regions.

In an almost inaccessible place, to which one goes by a narrow, winding, little known path, is found (or was found) a shelter made with large wooden pillars, or other smaller posts, supporting a roof made of *cogon*. All of the building materials have been obtained without the use of a cutting implement of iron, steel, wood, or stone. The hand of man and luck should build all of the buildings or *camarín*.[166] *Cogon* felled without tools of any sort, using only the strength of one's hands, and trees found in the countryside, topped to the ground by the typhoon, by the action of time or accidental fire, serve to build the pagan temple. Bindings of *balágon*,[167] obtained in the same manner, fasten and support this work done by many.

---

[166] *Camarín* in Spanish refers to the place behind the altar where the church images are stored and ornaments are kept or to the dressing room of a theater. However, Echaúz (see Glossary) and others often use the term to mean *bodega* (storehouse or warehouse) when describing the buildings of a hacienda. *Kamarin* (Pan.) is a barn, shed, storehouse, etc., (Kaufmann n.d.:82). On the following page Echaúz appears to refer to a room where religious ceremonies are held.

[167] *Balágon* refers to any pliable tough root, stem, or vine used as a rope (Kaufmann n.d.:82).

Next to the *camarín* is a well of crystal clear water, surrounded at some distance by trees, shrubs, and plants of exhuberant growth. But they neither grow near the well nor shed their leaves into its mouth, according to the *babaylanes*, because of the supernatural effect of such pure and clear water.

The *camarín* and the well are located near the Balabago stream which flows through the mountains of Tubuñgan (Iloilo). Balabago flows always in a direction contrary to nature, or so the chiefs of the *babaylan* council swear. This site is witness to many *babaylan* adventures in which the learned members or *sabios bablianes* (as they are called in the mountain language) are givers of water, sun, good and bad weather by intimate contact with the spirits. Water from the well wets the dry thirsty throats of the dancing *sabios* whose shouts resound through the Philippine channels (*canales*) and seas.

The big meetings, the mountain Areopagus,[168] or the Sanhedrin[169] of the well-known curers (*medico-rurales*), are held to coincide with our Holy Week. On Wednesday, the entertainments arrive--gifts, food, men, women, and children from a multitude of Bisayan towns. Thursday, the ritual begins, with many gathering in the retreat of the *babaylanes*, outlaws (*tulisanes*), and masters of the forest. Curiously, the session continues on Friday, in a blend without equal, when they become mystic brothers in an undignified illicit cohabitation, indulging their laziness, lust, and gluttony. For Saturday, following their native fondness, there is a grand cockfight, in which the anisette of Capíz, rice beer (*pañgasi*),[170] and *tûba* flow in greater quantity than the water carried in the stream of Balabago.

A witness present at the meeting of 1874, held in the mountains of Tubuñgan, reported that more than a thousand people attended the sacrifices, and that the *terciados*,[171] *talibones*,[172] and spears (*lanzas*) they brought would not fit into four carts. In this year, the assembly was the cause of much admiration by both neophyte and initiated. The great "rabbis" officiated, the

---

[168] *Areópago montesco* refers to the Athenian areopagus that was the supreme tribunal of Greece. Hence, it refers to any tribunal with the authority to make binding decisions.

[169] The Sanhedrin was the ancient Jewish high court.

[170] See Glossary.

[171] The *terciado* is a *talibone*-like weapon. See also Glossary.

[172] The *talibon(g)* is a large, heavy bolo (Kaufmann n.d.:893).

Ingo[173] of Cabatuan, another *Ingo* from Baroc, jurisdiction of León, Julian, and some others. The Tatauans, Paels, and Pacios sent pigs.

When the catastrophe that took the life of Father Agustino [Calzado] occurred, Ramos was the great officiator, the keeper of the two printed books--the *babaylanes'* Vedas. They pointed to Ramos as the author of Calzado's death. Ramos paid for his crime, not in a penitentiary or in some public place of execution, but among the sacred trees, the lonely forest and jungle, untouched by a civilizing footprint, where the sun's rays never penetrate. He was assassinated by his cousin, Fruto, who beheaded him with one slashing blow of the bolo. Fruto died in Manila condemned for a criminal act that was motivated by a reward he did not enjoy.

Clouded and wrapped in the most complete obscurity, the origins of *babaylanism* can only be guessed. To acknowledge its links with some ancient civilization would not be desirable. Those who like to question or seek out the origins of races and sects find similarities. They speak of sayings, stories, and traditions; they doubt, vacillate, and write. But one thing is certain, most surely they will find nothing.

The *babaylan* has borrowed from some and imitated others. From this mixture is formed the ritual and liturgy that partakes of the primitive. It stresses, in its custom and habit, laziness, deceit, sleepiness, lasciviousness, independence, fondness for the solitude of the forest, and eating whenever possible.

They say that the idea of religion is innate in man, even in the most uncivilized people. But this is not true of this sect which in reality does not have a regular worship, taking it only in small doses for six years. Later, having gained courage during such an extended period of time, the members cram it all into a seventh year in a quantity which is excessive.

Whatever the *babaylan* practices, his activities cannot be called a religion. It is a baseless idea, a lucrative business exploited for its own benefit. It shares with and is related to some primitive races in the respect it pays to the moon and in the persistence of certain dances. But it does not possess the great love of and fervor for a divinity. It lacks such characteristic signs of religion as valor and spirit, desire to fight or a longing for death with honor. It does not ask for triumph or the crown of the laurel which the *babaylana hermosa* (priestess), descended from a hundred leaders, must wear on her brow. They are happy and have enough and more with

---

[173]*Ingo* is the nickname for Domingo.

the crown of *tûba-tûba*[174] if they have a headache.

The number seven figures in all their ceremonial acts. Seven pigs are sacrificed; each seven years reunions are held; and seven robes are burned. Seven times the cloths (*mantas*) are thrown into the fire, while the pig is jumped over seven times before it is killed with a dagger.

Now the *babaylanes* are gathered in the proper place. The leader (*mayor-mayor*[175] as the highest ranking of them all is called) is dressed in a black robe, wears a sash and a handkerchief of red. He is accompanied by two initiates who carry a tray with betel nut chews and tobacco to a table covered with cloths woven in Miagao [Panay]. On the table can be seen a pig's head with neither brains nor tongue, many lights, crabs, banana blossoms, roasted suckling pig, sweets, sugar and rice pastries.

The leader stands before the altar. He places on the altar a book the size of a Spanish dictionary. The first five pages of the book are printed in Latin, followed by a picture of the Eternal Father, and further followed by the Bisayan lesson in green, red, and black letters. They place a large earthenware jug of *tûba* and another of rice beer at the book's side.

Now they ask for a plate of coals into which the incense (*almâciga*)[176] is cast. The smoke rises. The leader touches the altar seven times with the dagger, throws it onto a round shield, and then seizes and waves it in the air. His feet begin to move; his eyes open and look as if they will leave their sockets. His body cannot rest. He calls the spirits, shouts, cries out, sweats, while the noise of the gong deafens the assembly.

Seven pigs are tied, awaiting the results of that grotesque pantomime. Seven leaps precede the beheading of the animals and, once dead, they go to the hands of the cooks who prepare and cook them to satisfy the hunger of so many people.

The leader rests a few minutes before continuing the procession to the sacred forest to leave food for the spirits. In this

---

[174] *Tûba-Tûba* (*Barringtonia racemosa* (Linn.)Blume) is a shrub or small tree with white or pink flowers that line a long stem (Brown 1957 3:53-54). It would be most appropriate for a "crown." In some parts of the Philippines the leaves of this plant are plastered to the temples as a headache cure.

[175] *Mayor-mayor* is the name given the leaders of the *babaylanes* (Romero 1974:168).

[176] *Almâciga* or Manila copal (*Agathis philippinensis* Warb.) is used throughout the Philippines as an incense (Brown 1957 1:53ff).

procession are all the *babaylanes* and *babaylanas* who offer sweets and other things to the spirits without any distinction so that they may be given everything they ask of them.

They eat and drink, passing the days and nights in confusion and in the most absolute communion. At a stated hour the seven cloths and seven robes will be burned and the seeds given. The leader talks with the spirits and, before the delivery of the refreshments and quantities of money, they return to their huts and places. A great escort accompanies the chief "rabbi" who, mounted on the sacred bull, cannot turn his eyes again to the place of sacrifices.

CHAPTER XVI

THE LOCUST

The locust is one of the greatest calamities that afflicts agriculture in the Philippine Islands.

Poor hacienda owners! Although he has not yet rested from the fatigue and weariness of a morning and afternoon of continual work, word comes that a band of locust has appeared near the hacienda. The news comes from the field where they cut the cane to the field where they plow or plant. It comes also from the mill-house to the warehouse, from the pier to the house, and to the square where the *bagasse* dries. Workers, women, and foremen--as carriers of bad news all of them are effective--hasten to spread the information.

It is a question of the hacienda owner's temperament. Some shrug their shoulders and with stoic calm and self-control, very possessed and nerveless, without exclamations, say: "Ah. Patience--no more." Others stretch, squirm, are moved and affected, and put their hacienda under a state of siege, charging the smartest of the foremen and workers with the proclamation of martial law. Empty oil drums, split bamboo, and cowbells--anything that can make noise or smoke--are readied without losing a minute.

It is three in the afternoon. The sun levels with its rays; the carts and oxen go at a languid and monotonous pace. The carabao plow, the mill shreds the cane, the caldrons boil and. . . all are paralyzed at the violent sound of the bell. In its haste it asks aid, cries help, and in this way makes the workers understand that all should hurry to the same place, leaving their jobs.

At the extreme south of the hacienda a north wind now blows. It is known that the locust always travel at a distance from and in a direction contrary to the prevailing wind. There is a cloud, many clouds, like smoke about to vanish. A dense fog interposes itself between the earth and the sun. The formation of locusts advances rapidly, slows a moment, and wavers in its direction, impeded by the smoke from the burning of great piles of slightly dampened dry brush and *cogon* grass. Finding the place occupied by the heads, or the guides, of the locust band, women with flags, little ones, workers, dispatchers, and anybody not busy in the area are provided with anything that makes noise to fight the band and to change its direction.

Within the limits of the hacienda, the locusts rest in planted fields or in the new cane fields. In minutes the green and luxuriant growth of the plants disappear, eaten by these destructive insects. In some haciendas the locusts are fought with cords stretched across the field from side to side to hinder them, especially in places where the harm and destruction caused would be considerable. If in spite of the good efforts used, the locust spend the night and lay their eggs, the work that comes with the appearance of their young (*locton*)[177] is multiplied excessively.

The young locusts quickly come out in an unknown manner of the ground within nine to twenty days after the eggs are laid, depending on the weather. Then they begin to cause damage, traveling and following the route begun by the first of those who emerged from the ground. The hard working farmer follows and kills the small insects, interrupting their path, defending the plantings they are about to attack with flat, smooth pieces of galvanized iron. The locusts are guided in their path with flags--dry leaves from trees or any other object that catches the wind--to depressions in the ground some distance away. On the edges of the depressions are placed pieces of slippery banana [stalks] which will cause the insects to slip to the bottom. The insects are then covered with dirt, tramped down, and a fire is built on the spot.[178]

---

[177]Kaufmann does not list *locton* (or any of its possible variations). However, *lúkton* in Cebuan, is the young of the locust called *dulon* (Hermosisima and Lopez 1966:296).

[178]Echaúz describes the rules for fighting locusts in *El Porvenir de Bisayas* (June 8, 1890), a periodical published in Iloilo.

CHAPTER XVII

FIGURES CONCERNING SUGAR, ABACA, AND ABACA CLOTH (*PACOL*)

A mistaken idea has been (and still is) commonly held regarding the agricultural operations of a hacienda on the island of Negros. This false notion comes from superficial and inaccurate studies stemming from lack of knowledge of the scarcely visited province. The crops that produce its overflowing abundance and money are represented by the Chinese plow.

An accounting of the expenses of a well-run and properly administered hacienda will clearly show the regular and necessary expenses involved. Consider the accounts of a hacienda that has not borrowed money at twenty to thirty percent and has not used the contract loan, a procedure that consists of accepting money to repay it later in sugar, losing three or four *reales fuertes* [a *pico*?] or more of its market value. Such an accounting does not consider extraordinary expenses which occur as a result of bad weather, of some calamity, epidemic, or flight of workers--happenings that are quite frequent in these latitudes.

Patents for the mill, with their extra charges, are neither entered nor charged. Excluded [from the following table] are the two and one-half percent sales commission, the salaries of the machinist, drying, sacks, tare, etc. An attempt has been made to strike an average in some details. In almost all these figures, the hacienda is considered to have a good location, roads, and favorable transportation.

Take as given a hacienda of 220 or 240 *hectares* of land, supplied with enough animals, machinery, buildings, carts and other equipment, and is producing some 7,000 *picos* of sugar.

Salaries of foremen, overseers, and wage expenses for one year.............	$ 3,600.00 [pesos]
First cultivation of one hundred *hectares* of land; seven plowings at one peso[179]/*hectare*/plowing...........	700.00
25,000 sugar cane points at 1-7/8 pesos/ *hectare*................................	187.50
Two weedings at three pesos/*hectare*......	300.00
Secondary work in the cane...............	700.00
Cleaning of canals and ditches...........	600.00
Cutting and hauling of the cane to the mill room (carts and animals furnished by the agriculturist) at 0.5 pesos/*pico*	4,375.00
Firewood for one hundred days of milling at eight pesos/day.....................	800.00
Collection, carrying, and drying of the *bagasse*, twelve workers a day..........	250.00
Packing of sugar and stacking of 14,000 sacks at one peso/100..................	140.00
14,000 sacks of 1/2 *pico* each delivered to the hacienda at 3-1/2 pesos/100.....	490.00
28,000 rattans delivered to the hacienda at 2-1/2 peso [per one thousand].......	70.00
Transportation to the wharf at 1/2 *real*/ *pico*..................................	437.50
Loading at one *céntimo*/*pico*..............	70.00
Freight for 7,000 *picos* at one *real*......	875.00
Expenses in Iloilo at two *céntimos*/*pico*..	140.00
Grease, paints, and gaskets for machinery	100.00
	[$13,835.00][180]

Beginning in 1887 and 1888, when the prices of sugar fell and the rains did great damage to the cane, the planting of abaca today is not neglected in the new lands of the interior. Here it grows more productively than on the lands along the seashore. Negros is profiting from this variety of crops, necessary for the prosperity of the hacienda owners, and by this demand for its excellent

[179]The abbreviation pfs. has been translated as pesos. It could also be translated as *fuertes* (Cuyás 1940:520).

[180]In this table Echaúz sometimes lists the cost based on 100 *hectares* (e.g., plowing, weeding, etc.), not 220 *hectares*.

lands. The following data add to what could be said about this important fiber.

These are the figures [below] for planting twenty *cavanes* of abaca, the cost and time necessary for its cultivation, and the approximate results. For a twenty *cavan* planting, 72,000 abaca cuttings (*pies*) are used. Once in production (or within two years) each will give one plus or two more pounds of clean fiber for a total of 1,047 *picos*. Figuring the sales price for this amount at eight pesos for one *pico* adds up to 8,376 pesos.

EXPENSES OF INSTALLATION

For twenty *cavanes* of mountainous [uncleared] land at twenty pesos [a *cavan*], if it is purchased.........	$ 400.00
Clearing of the same amount of land.....	400.00
Purchase of 72,000 plants at $15/1,000..	1,080.00
Cleaning and cutting with bolo at $16 [per *cavan*]..............................	320.00
Equipment and warehouses for processing.	300.00
One-half of the output for the cultivators............................	4,188.00
For interest for two years on invested capital................................	500.00
	[$7,188.00]

Comparison

Production..............................	$8,376.00
Cost of production......................	7,188.00
Favorable balance.......................	$1,188.00

If the worker, instead of being given one-half of the output, were to be paid a wage of two *reales fuertes* a day, and needing forty men for 240 days of work, this would cost only $2,400 for the cultivation, and would result in $1,788 more for the proprietor. Each *cavan* would produce 52 *picos*, 37 *cates*,[181] for $418.80 *céntimos*.

These figures are for the first years. In later years there is no expense other than the $320 for the clearing and the share to the farmer. In following years, the cultivation can continue without interruption, inasmuch as the plant reaches maturity in eight months, with production increasing later by twenty-five

[181]A *cate* or *catty* is a weight equal to 0.633 kilograms (Manila 1905 4:449).

percent. Supposing in this only one-half the calculated amount, a deficit of $906 will appear in the first year, a surplus of $1,634 the second year, and in the following years a surplus of $2,069.

It is interesting to note in this book that a few years ago an important foreign firm of Iloilo advertised for and promised to pay five dollars per *pico* for the finest quality of fiber obtained from the *pacol*. It intended to show with this price its great support of the cultivation of *pacol*. This product, of the same ancestry and origin as abaca, is grown and woven in Ilog and Cauayan in southwestern Negros.

Now sixty-five *varas* of woven *pacol* weighs forty-six ounces or two pounds, fourteen ounces. The price for five *varas* that makes 576 rolls of five *varas* each, which at two pesos per roll, on the average, will bring a total of 1,152 pesos. If one-half of the product is given the workers, the total is 576 pesos. *Pacol* would then be worth 4.02-3/8 pesos per pound.

This shows how the value, profit, price, and esteem of *pacol* was probably perceived.

There is great interest in the island of Negros about the introduction and development of the cultivation of coffee. It is worth writing about as a reminder and a stimulus for the future if, at some time, growers trying new crops suffer failure or are discouraged in their enterprise in the fields because of calamities which no one could prevent in spite of well-thought out plans.

In 1840 Don Luis Guiquin, property owner and neighbor of Bacolod, had on his Hacienda Lupit a robust coffee tree which, in its extraordinary development, bore fruits that caught the attention of all who visited his place. Agustin Balseras, a Filipino native of Loygoy (now Granada), saw the coffee tree full of red beans like cherries. He asked the owner for half a dozen of the beans, with the idea of growing and multiplying them. The owner gladly acceded to this request. Balseras picked eight of the red berries which he stuck in the band inside his hat. He returned to his house in the forest between La Concepción and Granada. There Balseras planted the seeds. After a short time he had seven leafy coffee trees that soon were providing more than enough coffee for his own use and that of his family.

In 1862 a Recollect priest from Minuluan bought five *cavanes* of coffee beans harvested from Balseras' property. The priest planted them in seed beds (which he had built with his own funds). When they were strong enough to be transplanted, he distributed the seedlings to the houses, barrios, and sitios of La Concepción, San Fernando, Dos Hermanas, and Granada. These plants now form the coffee plantations which provoke and incite the continuation of the work begun on such a small scale in 1840 and followed with enthusiasm and generosity in 1862. Coffee cultivation is effectively carried forward today in the barrios of Alig, Alegría, Sta. Rosa, and in various towns of the western region of Negros.

The new lands where the missions must take root invite the exploitation of this estimable tree. But it should not be forgotten that diversification of crops, above all those which do not require great expense and which give quick and certain yields, is what builds the happy and sure progress of growing towns.

CHAPTER XVIII

A WAKE ON A BISAYAN ISLAND

Along a road made narrow by luxuriant bamboo and in a small plaza where grass (*bugang*)[182] and the yellow-flowered purslane (*verdolaga*)[183] grow is a long, narrow nipa house. It is not as well made as those of Sicaba and Cápiz. At one side is a vegetable garden and orchard as well as a flower garden where eight banana trees grow, a guava tree, and fourteen taro plants. Bushes ring a well whose water, taken out with a bamboo bucket (*timba*)[184] and a rattan cord, serves for bathing the inhabitants of the house and those in the vicinity.

Ascend--better, clamber up--to the house by a ladder made of two bamboos to which six wooden steps have been lashed with rattan. This gives access to a stairlanding or balcony where are a big basket (*tabig*)[185] containing peas (*cadios*)[186] and mongo beans (*balatong*),[187] the hearth, a pair of pants and a hat new since the typhoon of '83 when *Capitán* Ingo was *gobernadorcillo*. There is also a dog with her seven thin pups, a

---

[182]*Bugang* (*Phragmites vulgaris* (Lam.) Trin.) is a grass used to make a "peculiar type of dust broom used for sweeping highly polished floors" (Brown 1957 1:165).

[183]A species of *Portulaca oleracea*.

[184]*Timba* is a bucket or pail used to draw water from a well (Kaufmann n.d.:928).

[185]*Tabig* is "the ordinary rice harvesting basket made of bamboo splints" (Kaufmann n.d.:874).

[186]*Cadios* or *kadios* (*Cajanus cajan* (Linn.) Millsp.) is the pigeon pea (Brown 1957 2:97).

[187]*Balatong* is the *mungo* (mongo) bean (*Phaseolus aureus* Roxb.) (Brown 1957 2:137).

drinking water jar (*bañga*)[188] inside the *salángsang*[189] fastened to the wall, and the valued bamboo settee (*langcape*) which is used for sleeping, siestas, and naps where the best and most of the hours of the day are spent.

The parlor remains separated from the balcony by a door of heavily matted nipa, in some places reinforced with crossbars of bamboo laced with a fine vine (*náui*).[190] On entering the door the first things that come to the eye to be admired are a loom of *molave* wood [for weaving abaca cloth] ready to be used, two tied fighting cocks, a stool, an oil lamp (*tinghoy*),[191] two mats (*amacanes*), the mortar for pounding rice, two bolos (*binañgon*), a box with an Adolph hat, and some Chinese shoes from Macao hanging from the roof ridge. There are a number of chicken nests (*pugarân* or *pugadân*) for the hens, a half used pair of socks, various images and pictures, and a suitcase where the best clothing is kept. There are also a chair, the harness (*gota*) of the carabao, the rope or plowline (*guicos*), and the sybaritic hammock (*duyan-duyan*) made with rice sacks and hung from the houseposts with *burí* rope.

Under this room in what is called the *silong* [space under the piled dwelling] are seen a plow, carabao, hen with nine chicks, a rake, two consumptive pigs, one of them tied by the ear to a housepost or beam of the house, and the second secured at the belly by another rope tied to the crossbeams under the floor of the room above.

It is seven at night, and the parlor is too small for the many visitors who keep arriving. There is no exterior or interior sign to signal happiness or merry making, but there are signs of sadness. Instead of the accordion and guitar (*buctot*), there are funeral crepe and widow's weeds. There are weeping, sighs, and a novena for the soul which had been started on its way the day before. The prayers are for the soul of *Alguacil* [Sp. constable or peace officer] Itoy, owner of the house, who was buried two days earlier in the town's cemetery.

The hearth which for months before scarcely had any fire, now smokes, burns, or sparks, fed by great amounts of mangrove firewood (*bacjao* or *bakhau*). Near the hearth, the cook of the

---

[188] *Bañga* is an earthenware jar used to store and cool drinking water (Kaufmann n.d.:96).

[189] *Salángsang* is a "length of bamboo split down to a certain depth into narrow strips and opened out like a basket. It is used as a stand for pots, water cooling jars, etc." (Kaufmann n.d.:808). Also see Glossary.

[190] *Náui* or *nito* (*Lygodium* spp.) is a vining fern used for tieing and weaving purposes (Brown 1957 1:37-38).

[191] *Tinghoy* is "A small pan or bowl filled with coconut oil and used as a lamp" (Kaufmann n.d.:934).

barrio leader, Tinoy, generously loaned by his employer for these nights, prepares in kettles and frying pans, the *quinilao*,[192] *alicomo*,[193] Chinese vermicelli (*sotanghon*), rice noodles (*pansit*), fried fish mixed with vinegar and spices (*escabeche* or *eskabetse*), pork (*babuy*), stew (Sp. *estofado*), *paccio* [*pako*] and other dishes of the Filipino lower class cuisine.

Following custom, the prayer is begun, the rosary said, and then the novena for the souls is recited. When these are finished, all are seated on the floor in the parlor. On the bamboo mats, put there for this purpose, are placed many platters and bowls of full of food, rice, and cups [*tabos*][194] of *tûba*. They eat with their hands, without spoons and forks, until they are satisfied and full.

When this interesting task was done, the men approached a representative of the house to ask permission to play the games that usage and habit have established in families devoted to tradition. This custom has vanished now among most inhabitants of the Island.

Once permission is granted, the players sit in democratic concord in the presidential office, or, that is, on the floor on a mat made in the factory at Victorias. The players are those who take the role of the king (*rey*), his consort, the queen (*reyna*), the *espadilla* (wooden sword) in the center, and the *bellacos* (male villains) to the right of the king and the *bellacas* (female villains) to the left of the king.

The king orders but does not execute. He who is installed in this elective office should be the slyest and craftiest of the group. He should have spent some years in the public tribunal or served voluntarily as a scribe in the government, a pacified region (*alcaldia*), or the administration. The second person, or the wooden sword, with a rattan whip in hand, is the executing arm for the orders of the king. He should be very smart, too smart. The *bellacos* and *bellacas* do what they are ordered. If they do not they are punished with blows [of the whip] or required to improvise a *loa*[195] or speech.

---

[192]*Quinilao* is a raw fish prepared with vinegar and spices.

[193]In Cebuan, *alicomo* (*alikúmu*) is a sea crab that is not usually eaten (Wolff 1972 1:25). However, these small crabs sometimes are found in the markets of Negros Occidental.

[194]*Tabo* is a cup made from the coconut shell.

[195]*Loa* or *lua* is defined as "A recitation, recital, declamation; to recite or quote from memory some verses, or the like" (Kaufmann n.d.:514). In southern Negros Oriental this game was known and *lua* (or *luwa*) were verses recited by the participants, often at wakes. See Hart 1975.

When each is in his place the king begins the game by putting his open hands on the floor and says "*culasisi ang hari*" (the king will question). In this way he calls the attention of the *bellacos* and *bellacas* and warns them that the game is to begin.

Now the game. The king raises his hands to his head and lowers them to the ground, crying "*ang pato nagalupad*" (the duck is flying). Everyone would repeat these words and actions. If someone fails, the wooden sword turns loose a couple of blows, or the delinquent is obliged to recite the aforementioned *loa*, a model of its kind for the comparisons, histories, crimes, and tales it relates.

When this is finished, the king orders the execution of the *ate-ate sa buquid* [*búkid*], the black man [Negrito] of the mountain, which consists in having the *bellacos* and *bellacas* stand up, clasping their hands, sing and dance at the same time, making turns before the queen. Then he gives another order, a bit daring, in which the *bellacas* are obliged to climb the beams of the walls, chased by the *bellacos*. When the women are caught they are made to pound rice in the mortar for punishment.

They also play a game called "*La Pobrecita*" ("Poor little thing")--an innocent distraction which may become a sly pastime because of the rascality of the wooden swordsman who is a clever inventor of other diversions during the time of the novena.

CHAPTER XIX

THREE UNUSUAL PORTRAITS OF NATIVES TAKEN FROM NATURE

There is no wish to make a portrait of true effigy of the *respectable* class that gets up at four in the morning and goes to bed at nine in the evening after work. There is no wish to present these persons who again and again with arguments and shouts move fifty, sixty, or a hundred workers. This photograph is taken directly from life; it is unique and applies to a single case.

Cabo-cabo[196] Mingoy has, as signs of his official identification, a face, feet, hands, nose, eyes, arms, and legs of an ordinary person. His chest is also ordinary. That deals with his physique. In regard to his morals, the irregularities add up to more than the ordinary.

He commands and ordains the life and soul of the small hacienda. He is the factotum, the one who knows all he should know, the one who overlooks nothing. The *corridos*,[197] the lists of workers, the books of devotion and spicy stories--all he devours.

He writes with ease and understands quickly; he knows the rules of addition for himself and the rules of subtraction for the workers. He knows how to handle the adze and chisel, plays

---

[196] *Cabo* or *Cabo-cabo* (Pan. *Kabo-kabo*) is a "petty chief" (Kaufmann n.d.:357). He was the person on the hacienda to whom the workers reported for daily assignments in the fields or the mill. *Cabo-cabo* and *encargado* (the latter is the individual who runs the hacienda in the absence of its owner) are terms used today in Negros Occidental (Lynch 1970:6).

[197] A *corrido* is a metrical romance of eight syllable verses based on plots of European origin (Maring and Maring 1973:117).

the guitar, sings *zarzuela*[198] verses and *balítaw* [199] and dances the *rigodón*[200] as well as the *lulay*.[201] It is true he is an expert in the art of love which he intuitively has learned. That is not a strange thing in one who lives from rags to riches, who benefits from the advantages of the worker and yet enjoys the privileges of the house of the hacienda.

At dawn and at dusk, *Cabo-cabo* Mingoy sounds the bell, calls the roll with a thundering voice, distributes the work of the hacienda, and puts marks where he should not. He gains but not without giving hours or rest at an agreed upon price or for favors received beforehand. Nobody calls him by his first name; he adds the last. He sells protection which one understands when he puts his left hand on the shoulder of his protégé or assigns him to the least heavy labor. His wage is double that of the workers to which he adds a stipend by supplying drinks, food, betel chews, or cards, thus keeping the proper order of things and satisfying his desires to acquire money which is not his.

He goes to the field if it strikes his fancy in cloth slippers (*chinelas*) and with an umbrella for rain or a parasol for sun, stays a little while at the work, and then goes to another place of work. In this peregrination, he goes to the field being planted for four to six turns of the plow and then very calmly enters some house where he dries his sweat or smokes, distracted in the contemplation of some beauty.

With a European saddle, mounted on a small horse of no value, he accompanies his bosses to town or to nearby haciendas and watches over the fighting cocks bound for fiestas of the greatest renown. During the cockfight he does not lose sight of the cocks in the hands of the trusted servants. It is *Cabo-cabo* Mingoy who sends them to the circle for the pairing or calls together the handlers. He holds the sheath given him by the handler while the cockfight is going on. He collects the money if the cock wins and pays if it does not.

---

[198]A *zarzuela* (*sarsuela*) is a variety of musical comedy (introduced by the Spaniards) with three acts enlivened by a cast and chorus singing folk songs and performing folk dances (Eggan 1956 3:1133).

[199]*Balítaw* is "An action-song, singing and dancing combined, a song accompanied by expressive gesticulations. . ." (Kaufmann n.d.:92).

[200]*Rigodón* is "A kind of dance; quadrille" (Kaufmann n.d.: 787).

[201]*Lulay*, according to the Glossary, is a "Philippine song and dance."

Knowledgeable of the lands of the hacienda, he consults his bosses in passing (as a courtesy) about the work of the following day. After a short conversation, he handles a number of civil matters (and other matters not civil), reads letters, writes, keeps accounts, and officiates once in a while as a Cupid without bow and arrow.

He is responsible in his action. On occasion, he is the intermediary between the worker who asks something for his sick mother, dead father or uncle, and the owner who pays. When the mood strikes him, he implores or menaces. On occasions he inspects with greater thoroughness than that indicated in the penal code--at least punishment by lashes does not appear in its pages.

Skilled in a certain class of discussions, he claims for his hacienda all the *perdigachos*[202] at its [mill] edges, and even from farther away. He knows the markets, games, and places where workers from the other haciendas gather--knows them like the palm of his hand. He frequents these places on Sundays and during the customary fiestas. He joins the workers in conversation, lures and seduces them, and concludes with flattering promises to get them to work on the properties of his boss. This does serious injury to the other owners. Sometimes he tries this with workers who know his tricks and is found with a kick sovereignly administered.

If the opportunity comes at a dance he stands face-to-face with his boss or a *teniente* of the public tribunal, wearing an *Americana* [a man's coat of American or European style] of a cut equal to that of the owner's son. He imitates this son in the width or narrowness of his trousers and in the length and cut of his sideburns which he wishes to have considered the handsomest of the hacienda. He imitates their greetings of head and hands.

He distributes rice among the workers which always results in a reduced quantity, something similar to the miracle of the Loaves and Fishes. His control of that cereal brings him friends and he gives them the most. When the owner complains about how quickly it is used, he always attributes the loss to robbery, mice, or some other simple and innocent cause.

Since he is manager of a hacienda where women work pulling weeds, seedlings, and cleaning the harvest, he must go there to look, observe, and study to appreciate the merit of the saying, "We have planted enough, milled enough, now let us go to pay the debt."

The *mediquillo* Busio, curer of great fame, [and others like him], fortunately are disappearing from the scene, allowing the

---

[202]Particles of hardened massecuite that have escaped pulverizing or grain separation by the *azucareros*.

spread of knowledge acquired through study and practice. He beats a retreat, but every now and then reappears to enter the pages of some criminal process [to be prosecuted] or to send a patient to the cemetery. Only rarely does he cure.

His therapeutic skills are very limited, curing all illnesses of *fasmo* or *pásmo*,[203] fever (*himanat*), cold or heat (*hangin*[204] or *cainit* [*kainit*]), and diarrhea (*panlibang*).

His method of curing new and rare sins.

When an unfortunate one has been attacked (as the *mediquillo* of *pásmo* says) by something which includes rheum, paralysis, and many other unknown things, and without asking its history, observing the patient's temperament,[205] of any of the very necessary preliminaries, he orders [a piece of green *burí*] to be put on the fire. After it is heated, it is wrung out, and the drops are mixed with salt. The patient drinks this mixture. If he vomits the prognosis is good because the evil humors are dispelled; if he does not vomit, the illness is serious.

He cures diarrhea with ginger and charcoal from the hearth. For a "cold stomach" he makes a poultice of pieces of a swamp tree, a tobacco stub, ginger, *aremisa*[206] and *buligan*[207] which is applied to the abdomen of the patient.

The curing of a dog bite is worth telling. One of these animals sunk its teeth into the leg of a worker who came to Busio to be cured. Busio gave him a preliminary examination. He then made

---

[203]*Pásmo* is an illness with such symptoms as "Spasms, convulsions; stiffness in the limbs with pain due to overexertion, or to exposure or to having caught a cold; a slight color or indisposition" (Kaufmann n.d.:731).

[204]Although *hangin* means wind, in this instance it means a cold wind.

[205]Temperament refers to the balance of hot and cold elements in the body; when they are not in balance, the person becomes ill. For an account of humoral pathology in the Bisayas, including Negros Occidental, see Hart 1969.

[206]*Aremisa* (*Artamiśa*) "A plant much used for medicinal purposes; wormwood, mugwort" (Kaufmann n.d.:58).

[207]*Buligan* may be the asparagus bean (*Psophocarpus tetragonolobus* Linn. D.C.). However, the Bisayan names for this plant are *kamaluson*, *segadilla*, and *sererella* (Brown 1957 2:160).

some holes in a *tandok*,[208] the tip of a cow's horn some four inches in length and open at the top. He applied this surgical instrument over the wound at its widest point, inhaled, and closed the holes with wax. It was left in place for three minutes while the patient whimpered and cried out "Woe is me" ("*Aragoy*"). The horn was removed, cleaned, and a poultice was applied to the wound. This poultice was made of ground deer horn, uncooked rice, and hair from the biting dog. All these ingredients were roasted, made into powder and then mixed with a little coconut oil.

Basio treats problems of the nerves, making some prodigious cures which have given him great fame. A young lady felt deprived of all movement and remained subject to an attack that left her body completely cold. She stayed in this state for five minutes, without any sign of improvement. Busio, struck by inspiration, ordered an iron used for ironing clothes to be prepared. He heated it, and the smoke [from the burning charcoal inside the iron] produced was sent over the face of the young lady. This medicine did not work. So Busio took the iron by its handle and carefully and lightly lifted the skirt, to lay it on the leg of the patient. But he stopped his efforts because when the iron fell on her flesh, a smell of grilled beefsteak and a prolonged "*Aragoy*!" told him that the senseless young lady had left that state in which she had been found.

We should not stop without pointing out that people like Busio are hidden enemies of all medical reputations, particularly those earned in the universities and of cures made through knowledge and good judgment. Through defamation and calumny Busio discredits the licensed practitioner or the doctor of medicine and surgery, taking advantage of his command of the language of the countryside. The Chinese *mediquillo*, another plague of the sick, and he usually quarrel and fight over patients. But they unite in speaking ill of the science of those who, by dint of experience, study, and title, properly practice it.

The *directorcillo*, Tisio, like the *mediquillo*, Busio, retreats to his lair, leaving room for new personnel. If they knew Tisio! You see him timid and fearful with the authorities, but arrogant, proud, and puffed with his own people. His sayings before them are commands, his phrases, citations, and his words, a summons. One of his questions is equivalent to an urgent order carried on horseback and requires a quick reply. His orders have the force of a sentence decreed plus the cost for the appellant.

---

[208]*Tandok* is "A cupping glass, a horn used as a cupping glass, a tube used for sucking blood from a wound" (Kaufmann n.d.:902).

He wears spectacles like an emperor in a street corner comedy. He arrives punctually at court and religious festivals dressed in trousers, an *Americana* coat, black tie, and hat. In his house, and before his family, he uses the authoritative tones of the court, recalling in this regard a mayor of the town of La Rioja who, everyday when he sat down to eat, said to his wife: "Look, Perpetua, you eat with the only Lordship in your town."

He has in his library the Escriche[?], the writs, the manual of the *gobernadorcillo*, the exercises of Rodriguez [?], the Philippics of the curia (*Curia Filípica*),[209] and Ovid's *Art of Love* translated into Spanish. He shows the books to his visitor (if he is the kind of visitor who travels in the country to learn) with the complacency of a two-year enlistee showing his fancy tasseled military hat (*morrión*) to one of his co-religionists.

Ignorant for lack of studiousness and of a lazy inclination, he files an occasional brief and believes himself to be a Pacheco.[210] He knows that there exist *Fuero Juzgo*,[211] *Las Partidas*,[212] and some other book or another, which were written by an idler for the torment of *directorcillos*.

It is not the aim of this work to link and relate Tisio and his kind with the directing officials of the courts and dependencies of the governments. They are helpful and modest functionaries and intelligent workers to whom one can entrust an issue, secure in the knowledge that it will be carried out perfectly.

---

[209]*Curia Filípica* is the name given to the four discourses of Demosthenes and Phillip II of Macedonia on the defense of the liberty of Athens. By extension, it also refers to the fourteen speeches of Cicero to Marc Anthony. And, by further extension, the phrase refers to any argumentative discourse or tirade.

[210]Pacheco may refer to Rodrigo Pacheco y Osorio, 15th Victory of Mexico (1624-1635).

[211]Until the seventh century two codes of law existed in medieval Spain--the law introduced by the Visigoths and the indigenous legal norms that were almost exclusively of Roman origin. In this century a fusion of these two legal codes occurred known as *Fuero Juzgo* (Marriman 1918 1:237).

[212]*Las Partidas* refers to the *Libro de las Leyes* which was the last and greatest legislative endeavor of King Alfonso X in the thirteenth century. The *Las Partidas* was the unification of Spanish law on a Roman basis. Since this legal code was divided into seven parts, it was also known as *Las Siete Partidas* (Marriman 1918 1:241).

The *directorcillo* sits in a favorite chair, dictates in a loud voice, chews, coughs, and sneezes--alarming symptoms of an organization less than organized. He hangs his spectacles on the end of his nose and his feet on the table. He orders in a rough voice from the deepest part of his throat, resting his chin on his chest. He has at his side rural police (*cuadrilleros*),[213] the head of these police, scribes, peace officers, interested parties, and sometimes the accompanying witnesses who sign their testimony as if it were for fallow land.

His writings are models of correctness and fairness, in the feeling of his partisans (for he, too, has supporters and commentators of his prowess).

"I have received the respectable order from Your Grace which I answered yesterday in my *esteemed* communication. . ." Sometimes he meddles as defender of the accused. He begins his long and diffuse defense, full of inadequate citations and commonplaces, with this prologue:

"Scarcely had the fair Febo [Phoebus] extended his golden thread (it was 11 o'clock in the morning). . ."

In a declarative judgment of some importance (it was a contract whose cancellation caused great harm), in his written argument of response using a *sublimated* style he says: "My surprise in reading the foregoing arguments was so great that it is comparable only that of the protagonist in *Playing with Fire* when he says, 'Duchess Medina, you swore love to me, and here I myself find you in the arms of another man.'"

To conclude. A *directorcillo*, to wit, Tisio, went to the governing house in 1884 to ask permission to give a sentence of up to twenty-five lashes for the theft of a *cavan* [of rice]. The Governor, who was indeed serious and rather grave but on some occasions joked, answered when he saw the insolence of the *directorcillo*: "Your claim is good. Ask it in writing and it will be given."

In five days the Governor opened a letter from the *gobernadorcillo* of the town where Tisio was the *directorcillo*. He was asking permission that the Governor condescend to concede the right to strike twenty-five blows with a rattan on the rump, adding "that now it has been used on a criminal in anticipation of that saving right."

---

[213]*Cuadrilleros* were guards who were stationed to protect the public buildings in the provincial capital and the towns.

CHAPTER XX

GENERAL CONSIDERATIONS

The island of Negros has abundant fertile lands with rich and ample drinking water, flowing rivers for the operation of machinery, and numerous valleys where thousands and thousands of cattle may graze. It is a producer second to none of sugar, of sufficient rice, abaca, and coffee. This island has a large working population and a multitude of individuals without occupations, the *sacadas* and non-Christians. It also has important problems to solve if it is to continue advancing as it has until now--if it is to realize legitimately based hopes. These problems are:

1. The question of the workers (*jornaleras*)
2. Missions
3. Roads

The problem of the lack of capital is omitted as is the question of high and rising interest rates. These must be solved in an essentially satisfactory manner if the three other problems reach a hoped for solution.

The Question of the Workers

This is perhaps the most important of the problems and transcends all the others because it alone can deter the progressive and florescent state of the province. The governing and the governed should give preferred attention to this important matter. The governing should hear and decide; the governed should put forth their ideas and be heard. The governed should search the archives for proposals that have been deferred, scarcely made public. Among these proposals are the statement of the Count of Cleonard on the *sacadas*, the projects of the Governor of Negros, Señor Subiza[214] [*sic*, Subinza], the project presented to a meeting in Silay in April of 1889 by a number of farmers from the town of Minuluan for a rural compound (*guardería*) for

[214]Eduardo Subinza was Governor of Negros from 1883(?) to 1885 (Cuesta 1974:142).

the workers, and the circular dictated by His Excellency Governor Valeriano Weyler, published in the *Manila Gazette (Gaceta de Manila)* on May 10, 1890.

The proposals for the regulation of workers by Señor Subiza [Subinza], the proposal for the compound from the town of Minuluan, and the circular of May 10, 1890, extracted and recombined to form workable propositions, and applied to the island of Negros in its domestic and foreign relations, could be the height of the expectations of the farmers.

In the concrete case of the workers of this province, two different aspects the problem presents should be studied. One aspect is the regulation of workers exclusively on and of the Island itself. The other aspect is the details and orders governing the recruitment of workers from nearby islands which should be easily and quickly resolved. The first aspect is worthy of consideration to avoid friction and legal intervention which at first glance, without probing deeper, will appear, in its character and attributes, an usurpation of rights. Thinking about it more carefully, this aspect should be brought under the jurisdiction of a properly legal body.

As has been seen, the question of day laborers (*bracero*) is not only that of the present. It has sprung from carefully thought out antecedents such as reports from farmers and experienced people including those who form the section of agriculture of the Association of this name and by the industry and commerce of the province of Iloilo. It has been considered in the unforgettable meeting of the *Círculo* of agriculturalists held in the capital of Panay, the second capital (in some eyes) of the Philippine archipelago [215]

All of the interested groups and all of the opinions, including the circular of May 10 [1890] in its second article, the regulations of Señor Subiza [Subinza], and the report of the section of agriculturalists (page 19)--and all that has been written on this point--agree in a very essential point. All these sources depart from a common idea that should save much work and give uncounted assistance. This is to give an identification card to the day worker or laborer in agriculture as the above cited circular recommended.

Every worker would always carry with him this card as a document of accreditation of his person. The identification card

---

[215]In April 1880 sixty hacienda owners met in Iloilo where they organized an association called *Círculo de Agricultores* of which Echaúz was nominated president. The by-laws of this club and news of the meeting were published in *El Porvenir de Bisayas* (Iloilo) September 6, 8, 11, and 15, 1888.

should be visa-ed and be on record in the offices and registry of the rural compound which should be established under conditions similar to those proposed by the people of Minuluan; that is the jurisdiction of each town should be divided in sections related to the boundaries of other towns.

Among the features of such an important service dedicated to the safe keeping of the fields and watching over the workers will be to make an extensive inquiry to find out the life styles of certain individuals. The statistics derived surely will uncover a scandalous number of persons without any trade or occupations. This will oblige the authorities to take serious measures and to propose acts destined to eliminate such unfortunate evils for agriculture.

On the cards will be written the terms and contractual obligations between hacienda owners and workers, adding to those published in the circular of May 10, 1890. The terms will be concerned with the kind of work, the wage to be received in the field, millhouse, or for other tasks, the hours of work, the number and kind of meals, travel expenses, discounts, the causes for deductions from wages, bonuses that may be received, and the customs and practices of the hacienda where they are going to work.

In the same way, the conditions of movement of workers from one province to another should be regulated in the direction of normalizing just laws of life and personal freedom, providing for pay and responsibilities. This will force the formation of necessary patterns directed to the end of knowing the accurate movement of the population. This is the fundamental basis for knowing which persons who inhabit the town are residents, transients, or neighbors, and those who are customarily subject to taking office and to paying the amounts indicated by the orders, rules, and laws.

All of the clashes that are provoked between the hacienda owners and workers could be resolved by unions which could be similar to those established by the Law of Waters (*Ley de Aguas*) of Spain. Wise, quick, summary, unappealable, and without cost, they take their origin from the *Tribunals de Aguas* of Valencia which are worthy models of imitation for their ease of administration, low cost, and promptness of the proceedings.[216]

Missions

After what has been written in the foregoing pages, there remains little more to be said in favor of such a useful and

[216]Echaúz proposed a plan to deal with these problems associated with sugar cane laborers that was published in *El Porvenir de Bisayas*, May 26, 28, and 30, 1890.

great project which will bring a Christian and social life to thousands of people.

With the economic question resolved by the missions themselves with income from the treasury, nothing can deter the creation of the missions unless it might be the details of procedure and formal administration, evaded in part, no doubt, by the activity in the office of the one who sends for the funds.

Of course, the *sacada* will pay for his card, and will be obliged to appear personally. But the same will not happen with respect to the non-Christians. Without disdaining the precepts of the Laws of the Indies (*Leyes de Indias*),[217] used with such successful application in other times, one must observe, a special conduct suitable to the non-Christian's application to work, conditions of sociability, and fondness for his new life and to the cultivation of the lands which he aids. These important problems must be left to the discretion and solution of the authorities and functionaries who live near him and can appreciate his disposition.

The creation of these missions will be the crowning of civilization in the island of Negros. It will be a spectacle that strikes the most reponsive chord in the heart of the true patriot. He will know that there exists an island of the Philippine archipelago whose slopes, valleys, canyons, mountains, and beaches are inhabited by Spaniards, and whose eastern and western regions receive the illuminating rays of the inextinguishable sun of Country and Religion.

Roads

[What are the] advantages of a railroad that includes the productive zones of the island of Negros? What conditions should it recognize: conditions of facility; technical matters and finance; length of the line; adoption of the route; and cost of construction?

One of the problems on which the development of the wealth of the Philippine archipelago depends concerns the facility, economy, and regularity of its communications. All matters that lead to this goal constitute considerable benefit to the public

---

[217]The Royal and Supreme Council of the Indies, located in Madrid, was organized to assume overall administrative and supervisory control of Latin America and the Philippines. All policies and laws for these overseas possessions were determined by the Council. In 1861 the Council codified the 400,000 edicts that had been issued into a *Recompilation of the Laws of the Indies*, reducing their number to about 6,400 (Schurz 1939:369).

interest and is an important business to he who understands this enterprise.

This statement is so evident that it would be useless to attempt to prove it, particularly with reference to the island of Negros and its interior which is limited to an agriculturally productive zone. There is no reason to question the expansion of crops that would be obtained with good roads when, in spite of having incomplete or impassable roads, or totally lacking them, wealth can be seen increasing prodigiously day by day. Considering roads, modern conditions require the use of that which assures communication. They make communication safe from all contingencies, and, at the same time, considerably lower the cost of transportation.

Railroads are referred to. If these means of communication are amply nourished with the funds they merit, commerce and industry will acquire greater importance and stability. Agricultural profits are naturally progressive, and bring with them many necessities which, in turn, generate greater trade.

The establishement of a railroad, even of limited size, will have sure results for the island of Negros. And if this line also goes to the interior, it will be of still greater advantage. It is a principle that when these ventures are considered, their worth is in direct relation to the distance from the coast because the waterways are fearful competitors.

An attempt is being made to establish communication among five towns in a rich and productive area with a rail line forty kilometers long through flat land which is suitable and in good condition for the installation and maintenance of the line. This land needs no extensive clearing or high embankments [along its rivers]. The difficulties are five river crossings which, when finished, will be permanent works of some importance. The point of departure of the railroad must be a good harbor, suitable for the export of goods to Iloilo. The opposite end of the line should be at a town in the interior, near the mountains, where cultivation presently ends but which offers extensive land for new crops.

So that all should be easy and advantageous, at the foot of the line (whose best route should be the object of technical studies) are to be found indispensable basic materials for the construction. There are first class woods in abundance, quarries and river beds to provide sufficient ballast. Brick can be made. In sum, there is no lack of those materials which are needed as basic elements for the construction of a railroad.

Two factors should be considered in deciding the success or failure of an enterprise of this type: population and production.

The line mentioned here directly and immediately effects 100,000 inhabitants. It must serve a trade which supposes, as an early average, the movement of 500,000 *picos* of sugar in one direction and 60,000 [*picos*] of produce in the other direction.

These are achievements that can be gained now and this day can be enjoyed. It is undeniable that the installation of roads to the interior, along with the establishment of the missions, will create a considerable growth of wealth whose limits are difficult to fix. With this facility of communication the population will flow. The movement of the population, and similar phenomenon, will operate together with production, extending cultivation, and following this, with a greater variety of crops.

In spite of this, it is advised that the figures on which such projects are based should be realistic because that which is needed for the adoption of an economical road with fixed and moveable equipment is solely and precisely to satisfy the needs of today. Under this supposition, the construction of this railroad would be cheap. In dealing with a new business one should take into account the obstinacy of local capital, accustomed to illusionary advantages and positive risks.

A railway with a narrow gauge, given the industrial competence which exists in Europe, putting aside the expenses of expropriation, will not require considerable resources. We feel sure that the same interests which are to benefit from it will help in the building of the enterprise, giving reproductive use to one part of its capital.

Forty kilometers of railroad could cost, at most, 200,000 pesos, returning a sure profit of 70,000 pesos capable of reaching 90,000 pesos within five years of its installation and operation. Optimism counts for nothing in these figures. It is certain that there are details and fundamentals lacking--that cannot be denied. But at the height of these omissions and defects, justified by the necessity of not lengthening this book, there exists, in addition to the testimony of numbers, the general instinct that comprehends the impact and importance of the business which it founds.

It is recognized by all that the railroad is needed. Nobody denies the powerful and decisive influence it would have in promoting the material interests of the island of Negros. The only factor missing is a determined will--a true mercantile spirit--that the railroad be built. Well understood mercantilism serves to conciliate foreign interests with one's own. In this regard, the railroad that has been discussed here will completely fulfill this objective.

CHAPTER XXI

FAREWELL TO THE ISLAND OF NEGROS

Now it is seen, still it is admired. So it seems to the sweating and burning brow when comes the perfumed air of the *ilang-ilang* [flower] of Malógo and the scents emanating from the *sampaguita doble*[218] and the gardenia planted in the garden by a loving hand. Now the peaks of Marapara and Canlaon are clear. In their foothills are based the progress and civilization of a working country. Their slopes still harbor savagery and barbarism to be dislodged from their lairs tomorrow by the plow which always advances in seeking new lands and by the missionary always anxious to complete his religious and patriotic duties.

Pontevedra, La Carlota, Candaguit!--living examples of the working man who had found recompense. Ilog, Kabankalan, Jimamylan, and Ginigaran!--faithful testimony to what can be accomplished when activity and energy directs the work of lazy and neglectful temperaments. Minuluan, Bacolod, Silay, Saravia, and Victorias!--permanent examples of the worth of an elderly Recollect priest [Cuenca] who laid out roads and who taught others how to make water-powered machines. Bais!--force without equal of a few Spaniards united in work. Hacienda owners all!--more than proof, a daily argument. You seem a perennial signal, attesting and putting to a manifesto the knowledge acquired through painful experience and intelligence gained from the continuing rains that annihilate our harvests and the locusts that raze our plants.

An island awakening in the Philippines, an island that at two or three in the morning launches into space a hundred steam whistles--sounds that proclaim the festival of work. The industriousness of its inhabitants merits being studied and understood. It merits being done justice and you, farmers of Negros, have not done that.

---

[218]*Sampaguita doble* (*Jasminum sambac* (Linn.) Ait.) is a fragrant white flower that often is mixed with *ilang-ilang* to make garlands (Brown 1957 3:221-22.

In a time not so far in the past, in that exhibition where our steam plows, tramways, engines of five cylinders, European and American plows, and the designs of our haciendas should have been admired, what was shown were only a crude house, a plow that barely scratched the earth, the black Calibas [Caliban or Negrito] whose name was changed for the more expressive and shorter Tek, and a sample of sugar conveniently arranged in a kitchen utensil.

From north to south, from Victorias to Ilog, from west to east, from one shore to another, from Malisbog to Guimbalaon, to San Fernando, to Granada to Cádiz Nuevo, to Murcia, to Zaragoza, to Bais, to La Castellana, to La Isabela, to Payao, to Dumaguete and to Nueva Valencia is an immense area [the farmers] wrestled from the swamp and the forest. These lands represent the work of little more than forty years. There is no point from which a person, indeed, no person himself who, stepping for the first time on the territory of Negros, can stop saluting, admiring, and thinking of the value of initiative well supported, of what this country could be. To this add the prodigious forces and influence of our brothers across the sea and those of this side who learn by example, who imitate when they see the benefits, who work, cooperate, and prosper as they see themselves changed into landowners.

Your royal road, disembarking in one of the many coves of the Island, speaks to the farmer and gives proof of its advantages for him. Your roads from the towns to the mountains and the highway (the only one of the Island) proclaim your active and enterprising life. Consider the new crops of coffee and abaca. Observe the opening of the land made by those who constantly seek their future, not in the distractions of cards, games, cocks, and laziness, but in productive tasks of a rich and fertile soil.

You have embraced with affection the Spaniards who have come to you and sprinkled your land with the sweat of their brow. To you come the fearless navigator who leaves the weariness of the sea for those no less of the field, the business man born in the south, the retired army man, and the one anxious to prosper, he who lives on the shore or who inhabits the mountains, the Filipino desirous of betterment, he of British, Swiss, and French nationality, and the daily worker who wants to pay his due. The provinces of Cápiz, Iloilo, and Antique send you their workers. England and America come with their steel tools, machines, and farm equipment. All live from you, Island privileged by your lands and industriousness. You have not bid farewell to anyone or does anyone who is not lazy or a bad worker feel ill-treated by you.

Your rivers that served as a nest and refuge for reptiles today run water-powered machines. They are now an element of prosperity. Such impetuous torrents in their courses, of beautiful passages and striking panoramas, whose floods to the sea are slowed and controlled, make a waterfall where shrubs, leaves and trees become a surprising example of unrivaled nature. Now your course is stilled in a tranquil pool where medicinal herbs grow on all sides. The waters are directed, by careful work carried out with perfection, to a narrow channel defended by a strong steel floodgate, well-secured against a subdued current.

Your roads are never lonely. Your rivers are always visited by the ships which come from Iloilo, the first city of the Bisayan islands. Your roads carry thousands of carts of cane and sugar on wheels and axles imported from Europe. The tramway battles with the rains, bad roads, and with loads surpassing the first ones. Wire fences surround the hacienda of Carmen. Fixed and permanent rails unite the wharf with Candaguit, La Fé, and La Carlota. There are steam plows on one hacienda after another; the canals bring water. You send to neighboring provinces thousands and thousands of pesos [earned] in those moments of worry and anxiety in September and October, hundreds of thousands of *picos* of sugar that the laborers plant, work, harvest, and process--in the midst of unskilled tasks. The battles and attempts with new crops--all this says with a single voice that you are the model island of the Philippine archipelago.

Adios! Island of the future.[219] Adios! Island where the Spaniard and the Filipino are fused in the most regenerative work of man--the cultivation of the land. Island of noble aspirations that guards in your breast the suffering sons of *el arado y del trabajo*. Island with isolated mountain peaks where you show, along with the white cap of Canlaon, an example of sugar factories that cheer and enchant the owner and he who visits and admires the country.

I hope that publication of this inaccurate book from my poor pen will present you truthfully. You are an example of the force and the struggle of man directed and carried to a noble end. You offer advice and lessons of what can be accomplished by the union of the immigrant Spaniard and the Filipino. How just it is to recognize the gifts and the conditions as one sees the haciendas where mixed names are heard with gratitude and respect. Together all march united by the beautiful bond of the brotherhood of Country. And from this to the defense of a holy idea and to the defense of work, the supreme aspiration of an honorable man.

---

[219]It is not known when Echaúz left the Philippines for the last time. He did return to Spain in June, 1890 (*El Porvenir de Bisayas*, June 8, 1890). This may have been the year he took young Enrique Magalona, a Filipino who had distinguished himself while studying in a seminary in Jaro, with him to Spain. Enrique, the son of Carlos Magalona of Saravia, married in Spain where he died (Varona 1938:Sixth Installment).

GLOSSARY

TERMS AND TRANSLATION OF SOME WORDS USED IN THIS BOOK

A

Abaca.............................. Fiber produced by one of the species of plantain.
Acsa.............................. Sharecropper of a hacienda.
Alili.............................. Usurious loans made in money to be returned in kind.
Alimbuyog.............................. The name given a rooster with black and red feathers, the former being more abundant than the second color.
Alisto.............................. Work which is customarily used to begin a task.
Amacan.............................. Matting made from the bark [*sic*] of the bamboo.
Ampajan [*Ampahan*]................. Fish of a superior class [*cavalla*].
Anting-anting...................... Amulet or charm.
Aragoy ó arogoy.................... Expression of pain, equivalent to "Woe is me!"

B

Babaye.............................. Woman.
Babuy.............................. Pig.
Bacjao.............................. Wood from the [mangrove] swamp.
Bâdlon.............................. A valuable fish [*pampano*].
Bagazo [*Bagasse*].................. The woody part [pulp] of the sugar cane after it has passed through the mill.
Baguio.............................. Cyclone. Hurricane [typhoon] of great intensity.
Baguis.............................. Shark.
Bajaque.............................. Loin cloth [or G-string].
Balatong.............................. Small French bean [mongo] of the country.
Banga.............................. Earthenware jar for keeping drinking water.
Bantay.............................. Guard or sentinel.

Baroto.......................... Small, narrow boat with a single hull and with bamboos tied on both sides to keep it from sinking [i.e., an outrigger].

Batulang.......................... A large basket.

Bayíbayí.......................... New rice cooked and mixed with sugar and the [grated] meat of young coconuts.

Bayon.......................... Sack made from the *burí* leaf tied with rattan for packing or keeping sugar and unhusked rice.

Bejuco.......................... A flexible and strong climbing plant [rattan] that grows in the forest; used to tie or bind objects.

Bilao.......................... Sifter woven from bamboo.

Binagul.......................... Sugar of the most inferior class.

Binañgon.......................... A bolo with a sharpened point.

Binuro.......................... Salted, pressed fish.

Bolo.......................... Pointed machete.

Bombon.......................... Internode of bamboo.

Bucay.......................... White.

Bugang.......................... A plant [reed-like grass: Kaufmann n.d.:137].

Bugsay.......................... Short oar, broad at the end that touches the water; it is used without being attached to the boat.

Burí.......................... A palm with a large trunk and leaves.

Butong-butong.......................... Molasses taken from the iron caldron at this stage, put into a bamboo and converted into sugar by hand.

Buyo.......................... Climbing vine whose heart-shaped leaves are mixed with a piece of the nut of a palm called *boñga* and lime from seashells; chewed by many Filipinos.

C

Cadios.......................... Lentils of the country.

Calan.......................... A small earthenware grate that serves for cooking.

Calayo.......................... Fire.

Camarín............................ A building for the intended storage of equipment [warehouse or storehouse].

Camasojon.......................... Name of a rooster with white and black feathers.

Camote............................. A white tuber similar to a potato [i.e., yam].

Carabao............................ The tame buffalo which is used in transport, hauling, and farm labor.

Carajay............................ Frying pan of the country.

Casaysayan sang mahal ñga Pasión ni Jesucristo........... History of the precious Passion of Jesus Christ.

Caua............................... Iron receptacle [or caldron] for cooking sugar cane juice. It is set on the top of the oven.

Cogon.............................. A grass that when dry is used to roof houses and storehouses.

D

Dindin pampango.................... Exterior or interior partitions of buildings made of woven bamboo or flexible wood, supported at intervals of a meter by a framework coated with lime and sand well mixed with water.

Duyan.............................. Hammock of rattan or cord.

F

Funcia............................. Public entertainment or fiesta.

G

Gabi............................... A very norishing white tuber [taro].

Gulay.............................. Any kind of cooked green vegetables.

H

Harigue............................ Wood posts that support buildings.

I

Ilang-ilang.................... A cultivated and wild tree which produces flowers from which is extracted an aromatic essence of this name.

Inuts.......................... The juice of the sugar cane. [Also an alcoholic beverage made of sugar cane juice: Romero 1974:13].

K

Kanoń.......................... Rice cooked in water.

L

Langcape....................... A bamboo settee.

Liplip......................... A whole *burí* leaf sewed with rattan.

Lison.......................... Fish with very tasty white meat.

Luguay......................... Tow rope of rattan.

Lulay.......................... A song and dance of the country.

Lusóng......................... Wooden mortar where rice is pounded.

M

Manglar........................ Lowland invaded by the sea [tidal swamp], where grow inferior woods such as *pagat-pat*, *bacjao*, *paigao*, and others and many shell fish. [*Mangle* is the mangrove tree].

Mecate......................... Rope of abaca or hemp.

N

Nipa........................... A low palm that grows in the [tidal] swamps. A distilled substance called *tûba* has industrial uses; its leaves serve as roofing and for outer walls of houses and warehouses. [See *tûba*].

O

Opus........................... Cigar or ciagrette stub or butt.

P

Pacalâs........................ An iron, wood, or bamboo rake.

Pagatpat....................... Wood of the swamp used in urban construction.

Palay.............................. Unhusked rice.
Palayas............................ *Media agua de los edificios.*
Panday............................. Worker employed as a mechanic. [Also means a carpenter or any skilled worker: Kaufmann n.d.:690].
Pangas............................. One way of planting rice.
Pañgasi............................ Wine made by soaking rice in water.
Parejo............................. Same.
Patadión........................... Piece of material three *varas* long by one and a half wide, sewn along one side, of varied colors and woven of cotton or silk. Serves as the garmet of the women of the town. It is wrapped around the body and fastened with a knot.
Petate............................. A smooth sleeping mat of the country, made from the leaves of a shrub [i.e., a reed called *ticug*].
Pilipig............................ Pounded soft [roasted] rice.
Ponot.............................. A fish trap built in the sea. It is made of bamboo, *palma brava* an other materials.
Pugarán............................ Chicken nest.
Pulá............................... Red.
Punque............................. A shoulder-borne bamboo litter for carrying an object.

R

Rompecandados...................... Fish resembling the hake [barracuda?].

S

Saláñgsang......................... Bamboo holder in which a jar is put to cool drinking water.
Salocot............................ Wide-brimmed hat.
Sampaguitas dobles................. A Climbing plant whose flowers are white and very fragrant and are similar to those of the jasmine.
Sampoc............................. To prepare the rooster for the fight.
Sapa............................... Creek.
Siantong........................... A bolo without a point.
Sijod.............................. Circular abaca fish net.
Silong............................. Ground space below the first floor of the house.

Soplado.......................... Derogatory name for a conceited or vain person.

Soplillo.......................... Furnace worker in the mill room.

Suallo.......................... Wooden block to press the sugar cane.

T

Tabás.......................... Rooster with white, pink, and reddish feathers.

Tabig.......................... Small basket.

Talibon.......................... A long bolo with a sharply pointed tip.

Talisayon.......................... A rooster with feathers a little darker than the *camasojon*.

Tanduay.......................... Liquor [rum].

Tangingui.......................... One of the best fish of these islands.

Tauo [*Tao*].......................... Man [or people].

Tericiado.......................... Weapon similar to the *tablibon*.

Tingui.......................... Market.

Timba.......................... A device to raise water [from a well].

Timsim.......................... Inner part of a plant used as a wick for coconut oil lamps.

Tira-tira.......................... See *Butong-butong*.

Tûba.......................... Liquor distilled [from the sap] of the coconut, nipa, *burí*, and *cabo negros* [palms]; subject to the method of distillation, it produces various classes of wine much valued by Filipinos.

U

Ubi.......................... A purple colored tuber that contains a large amount of flour.

Uay.......................... Rattan.

V

Varasvaras.......................... A mangrove swamp plant used to make fences.

BIBLIOGRAPHY

Agoncillo, Teodoro A. and Milagros C. Guerrero

1973 *History of the Filipino People.* Quezon City: R. P. Garcia Publishing Company.

Alicante, M. M. and others

1951 *Soil Survey of Negros Occidental Province, Philippines.* Manila: Bureau of Printing. Department of Agriculture and Natural Resources. Soil Report No. 14.

Brown, William H.

1954-57 *Useful Plants of the Philippines.* Manila: Bureau of Printing. Department of Agriculture and Natural Resources, Technical Bulletin 10. 3 vols. Reprint of earlier edition.

Corpuz, O. D.

1957 *The Bureaucracy in the Philippines.* Diliman, Quezon City: University of the Philippines.

Cuesta, O.A.R., Angel Martinez

1974 *Historia de la Isla de Negros, Filipinas: 1565-1898.* Madrid: Pontificia Universities Gregoriana Facultas Historiae Ecclesiasticae.

Cushner, Nicholas P.,S.J.

1971 *Spain in the Philippines. From Conquest to Revolution.* Quezon City: Ateneo de Manila. IPC Monographs, No. 1.

Cuyás, Arturo

1940 *Appleton's New English-Spanish and Spanish-English Dictionary.* Revised and enlarged by Antonio Llano. New York: D. Appleton-Century Company. 3rd edition.

Eggan, Fred (ed.)

1956 *Area Handbook of the Philippines.* New Haven, Conn: HRAF Press. 4 vols.

Gowing, Peter G.

1967 *Islands Under the Cross. The Story of the Church in the Philippines.* Manila: Philippines National Council of Churches.

Grossman, Theodore

1972 The *Guardia Civil* and Its Influence on Philippines Society. *Archiviniana*, December 2-7.

Hart, Donn V.

1956 *Securing Aquatic Products in Siaton Municipality, Negros Oriental Province, Philippines.* Manila: Bureau of Printing. Monograph of the Institute of Science and Technology.

1959 *The Cebuan Filipino Dwelling in Caticugan: Its Construction and Cultural Aspects.* New Haven, Conn.: Southeast Asia Studies, Yale University, Cultural Report Series.

1965a *'Tambal Para Sa Uhaw':* The Ethnography of the Buri Palm in Barrio Caticugan, Negros, Philippines. *The Philippine Journal of Science*, 94:339-72.

1965b From Pregnancy Through Birth in Bisayan Filipino Village. *In* Donn V. Hart, Phya Anuman Rajadhon and Richard J. Coughlin. *Southeast Asian Birth Customs: Three Studies in Human Reproduction.* New Haven, Conn.: HRAF Press: 1-113.

1967 Buhawi of the Bisayas: A Revitalization Movement and Legend-making in the Philippines. *In* Mario Zamora, ed., *Studies in Philippine Anthropology*: 366-396.

1969 *Bisayan Filipino and Malayan Humoral Pathology: A Study in Southeast Asian Ethnohistory and Folk Medicine.* Ithaca, New York: Cornell University, Southeast Asia Program. Data Paper 73.

1975 A Village Funeral: Death is the Friendly Foe. *Archipelago* 2:36-42.

Herre, Albert W. and Agustin F. Umali

1948 *English and Local Common Names of Philippine Fish.* Washington, D.C.: U.S. Department of Interior. Circular 14.

Hermosisima, Tomas V. and Pedro S. Lopez, Jr.

1966 *Dictionary Bisayan-English-Tagalog.* Manila: Pedro B. Ayuda and Company.

Kaufmann, Rev. J., M.H.M.

n.d. *Visayan-English Dictionary (Kapulúngan Binisayá-Iningl*í*s).* Iloilo, Philippines: La Editorial.

Larkin, John A.

1975 Review of Romero's *Negros Occidental Between Two Foreign Powers (1888-1900). Journal of Asian Studies* 35:174-175.

Ledesman, Antonio and others.

1971 *Liberation in Sugarland (Readings on Social Problems in the Sugar Industry).* Manila: Kilusan ng Bayang Pilipino.

Lynch, Frank, S.J.

1949 *An Mga Asuwang:* A Bicol Belief. *Philippine Social Sciences and Humanities Review* 14:401-427.

1970 *A Bittersweet Taste of Sugar. A Preliminary Report on the Sugar Industry in Negros Occidental.* Quezon City: Ateneo de Manila University Press. Institute of Philippine Culture.

Mallat de Bassilan, Jean B.

1846 *Les Philippines; histoire, geographie, moeurs, agriculture, industrie et commerce des colonies espagnoles dans L'oceanie.* Paris: Arthur Bertrand. 2 vols.

Manila

1905 "X. Systems of Measurement." *Census of the Philippines: 1903.* Manila: Bureau of Printing 4:447-455.

Marcos, José E.

1912 *Reseña Historica de la Isla de Negros Desde los Tiempos Mas Remotos Hasta Nuestros Dias.* Manila: La Vanguardia Press.

Maring, Ester G. and Joel M. Maring

1973 *Historical and Cultural Dictionary of the Philippines.* Metuchen, New Jersey: The Scarecrow Press, Inc.

Merriman, Roger B.

1918 *The Rise of the Spanish Empire in the Old World and in the New.* New York: MacMillan Company. 4 vols.

Motus, Cecile L.

1971 *Hiligaynon Dictionary.* Honolulu: University of Hawaii Press.

Phelan, John L.

1959 *The Hispanization of the Philippines. Spanish Aims and Filipino Responses,1565-1700.* Madison, Wisconsin: University of Wisconsin Press.

Reed, Robert R.

1967 *Hispanic Urbanism in the Philippines: A Study of the Impact of Church and State.* Manila: University of Manila. Reprint of original publication, *University of Manila Journal of East Asiatic Studies* 11.

Reyes, L. J.

1938 *Philippine Woods.* Manila: Bureau of Printing.

Romero, Ma. Fe Hernaez

1974 *Negros Occidental Between Two Foreign Powers (1888-1909).* Manila: Enterprise Publications, Inc. Published by the Negros Occidental Historical Commission.

Sa-onoy, Modesto P.

1972 *Binalbagan Centuries Ago.* Bacolod City, Philippines: Diamond Press.

Schurz, William L.

1939 *The Manila Galleon.* New York: E. P. Dutton.

Scott, William H.

1968 *A Critical Study of the Prehispanic Source Materials for the Study of Philippine History.* Manila: University of Santo Tomas.

Varona, Francisco

1938 *Negros: Historia Anecdotica de Su Riqueza y de Sus Hombres.* Manila: General Printing Press. 2 parts. [Translated by Raul L. Locsin. Serialized in the *Western Visayas Chronicle*, provincial supplement of the *Manila Chronicle*, June-September, 1965.]

Walker, Herbert S.

1910 *The Sugar Industry in the Island of Negros.* Manila: Bureau of Science, Bureau of Printing.

Wolff, John U.

1972 *A Dictionary of Cebuano Visayan.* Ithaca, New York: Southeast Asia Program, Cornell University. Data Paper Number 87. 2 vols.

INDEX

AFRICA PROGRAM
CENTER FOR INTERNATIONAL STUDIES
OHIO UNIVERSITY
ATHENS, OHIO 45701

ORDER FROM:
Ohio University Press
Scott Quad, Ohio University
Athens, Ohio 45701

Out of Print volumes (marked with an *) can be obtained in microfilm or xerographic copies from University Microfilms International, at Box 1467, Ann Arbor, Michigan 48106 or 18 Bedford Row, London WCIR 4EJ, England.

Publication Number:

1 - THE NEW ENGLISH OF THE ONITSHA CHAPBOOKS. By Harold Reeves Collins. 1968. 22 pp. $1.75

2 - DIRECTIONS IN GHANAIAN LINGUISTICS: A Brief Survey. By Paul F.A. Kotey. 1969. 20 pp. $1.75

3 - DEFINING NATIONAL PURPOSE IN LESOTHO. By Richard F. Weisfelder. 1961. 39 pp. $2.25

4 - RECENT AGRICULTURAL CHANGE EAST OF MOUNT KENYA. By Frank E. Bernard. 1969. 41 pp. $2.75

5 - THE STRUGGLE AGAINST SLEEPING SICKNESS IN NYASALAND AND NORTHERN RHODESIA, 1900-1922. By Norman H. Pollock. 1969. 21 pp. $1.75

6*- BOTSWANA AND ITS SOUTHERN NEIGHBOR: The Patterns of Linkage and the Options in Statecraft. By Richard Dale. 1969.

7 - WOLF COURTS GIRL: The Equivalence of Hunting and Mating in Bushman Thought. By Daniel F. McCall. 1970. 24 pp. $1.75

8 - MARKERS IN ENGLISH-INFLUENCED SWAHILI CONVERSATION. By Carol M. Eastman. 1970. 25 pp. $2.00

9*- THE TERRITORIAL EXPANSION OF THE NANDI OF KENYA, 1500-1905. By Bob J. Walter. 1970.

10 - SOME GEOGRAPHICAL ASPECTS OF WEST AFRICAN DEVELOPMENT. By R.J. Harrison Church. 1970. 34 pp. $2.75

11 - THE IMPACT OF THE PROTÉGÉ SYSTEM IN MOROCCO, 1800-1912. By Leland Bowie. 1970. 21 pp. $1.75

12 - MARKET DEVELOPMENT IN TRADITIONALLY MARKETLESS SOCIETIES: A Perspective on East Africa. By Charles M. Good. 1971. 39 pp. $3.00

13 - SOUTH AFRICA'S OUTWARD STRATEGY: A Foreign Policy Dilemma for the United States. By Larry W. Bowman. 1971. 1973 reprint. 32 pp. $2.50

14 - BANTU EDUCATION AND THE EDUCATION OF AFRICANS IN SOUTH AFRICA. By R. Hunt Davis, Jr. 1972. 60 pp. $3.50

15 - TOWARD A THEORY OF THE AFRICAN UPPER STRATUM IN SOUTH AFRICA. By Thomas E. Nyquist. 1972. 66 pp. $3.50

16 - THE BASOTHO MONARCHY: A Spent Force or a Dynamic Political Factor? By Richard F. Weisfelder. 1972. 66 pp. $4.50

17*- YORUBA PROVERBS: Translation and Annotation. By Bernth Lindfors and Oyekan Owomoyela. 1973.

18 - POST-MILITARY COUP STRATEGY IN UGANDA: Amin's Early Attempts to Consolidate Political Support. By Jeffrey T. Strate. 1973. 65 pp. $3.75

19 - HIGHLAND MOSAIC: A Critical Anthology of Ethiopian Literature in English. Compiled by Paul E. Huntsberger. 1973. 133 pp. $4.75

20 - THE KENYA NATIONAL YOUTH SERVICE: A Governmental Response to Young Political Activists. By Richard L. Coe. 1973. 39 pp. $2.50

21 - CONSTRAINTS ON THE EXPANSION OF COMMERCIAL AGRICULTURE: Iringa District, Tanzania. By Marilyn Silberfein. 1974. 59 pp. $3.50

22 - ECHO AND CHORUSES: "Ballad of the Cells" and Selected Shorter Poems. By Cosmo Pieterse. 1974. 75 pp. $3.75

23 - THE NIGER-NIGERIAN BOUNDARY, 1890-1906: A Study of Ethnic Frontiers and a Colonial Boundar. By Derrick J. Thom. 1975. 49 pp. $3.25

24 - A COMPREHENSIVE PERIODICAL BIBLIOGRAPHY OF NIGERIA, 1960-1970. Compiled by Edward Baum. 1975. 261 pp. $6.00

25 - ABYSSINIA TO ZONA AL SUR DEL DRAA: A Guide to the Political Units of Africa in the Period 1950-1974. Second Edition. By Eugene C. Kirchherr. 1975. 50 pp. $3.50

26 - THE ORIGINS AND DEVELOPMENT OF EFIK SETTLEMENTS IN SOUTHEASTERN NIGERIA. By Kannan K. Nair. 1975. 42 pp. $3.00

27 - MOUNTAIN WARRIORS: The Pre-Colonial Meru of Mt. Kenya. By Jeffrey Fadiman. 1976. 82 pp. Bib. $4.00

28 - DEPENDENCE AND UNDERDEVELOPMENT: The Development and Foreign Politics of Zambia. By Timothy M. Shaw. 1976. 67 pp. Bib. $3.75

29 - CHIEF EXECUTIVES IN BLACK AFRICA AND SOUTHEAST ASIA: A Descriptive Analysis of Social Background and Characteristics. By Edward Baum and Felix Gagliano. 1976. 43 pp. App. $3.00

30 - FEARS AND WORRIES OF NIGERIAN IGBO SECONDARY SCHOOL STUDENTS: An Empirical Psycho-Cultural Study. By Sadek H. Samaan and Anne J. Samaan. 1976. 90 pp. App., Bib. $4.50

31 - ISLAND OF THE BLEST: Islam in a Libyan Oasis Community. By John P. Mason. 1977. 173 pp. Index, Photos, Glossary. ISBN 0-89680-063-6. LC 77-620016. $6.00

32 - THE EARLY HISTORY OF NIUMI: Settlement and Foundation of a Mandinka State on the Gambia River. By Donald R. Wright. 1977. 122 pp. Maps, Glossary. ISBN 0-89680-064-4. LC 77-620032. $5.50

33 - DEFENSE LEGISLATION AND COMMUNAL POLITICS: The Evolution of a White South African Nation as Reflected in the Controversy over the Assignment of Armed Forces Abroad, 1912-1976. By Kenneth W. Grundy. 1978. 157 pp. ISBN 0-89680-065-2. LC 77-620051. $3.50

34 - COMMUNICATION FOR NEW LOYALTIES: African Soldiers' Songs. By Anthony Clayton. 1978. 64 pp. Photos. ISBN 0-89680-069-5. LC 78-17653. $3.50

ALSO: WEST/AFRICAN PIDGIN-ENGLISH: A Descriptive Linguistic Analysis with Texts and Glossary from the Cameroon Area. By Gilbert D. Schneider. 1969. 256 pp. $6.00

This book is an attempt to apply the basic principles of structural linquistics to West African Pidgin-English. After an introductory chapter which deals with the general characteristics of the language as spoken in the Cameroon area, the author proceeds to the treatment of sounds, meaningful units, and sentence patterns. A glossary and bibliography are included.

LATIN AMERICA PROGRAM
CENTER FOR INTERNATIONAL STUDIES
OHIO UNIVERSITY
ATHENS, OHIO 45701

ORDER FROM:
Ohio University Press
Scot Quad, Ohio University
Athens, Ohio 45701

Publication Number:

1 - THE MANDATE OF HISTORY AND CHILE'S FUTURE. By Eduardo Frei M. Translated by Miguel d'Escoto, M. M. Edited and Introduced by Thomas W. Walker. 1977. 85 pp. ISBN 0-8214-0334-6. LC 77-620018. $4.00

2 - MULTINATIONAL CORPORATIONS IN LATIN AMERICA: Private Rights and Public Responsibilities. Edited by Donald P. Irish. 1978. 135 pp. ISBN 0-89680-067-9. LC 77-620055. $5.50

3 - MULTINATIONAL CORPORATIONS AND INTERNATIONAL INVESTMENT IN LATIN AMERICA: A Selected and Annotated Bibliography. Compiled by Harold Molineu. 1978. 105 pp. ISBN 0-89680-068-7. LC 77-620052. $5.00

SOUTHEAST ASIA PROGRAM
CENTER FOR INTERNATIONAL STUDIES
OHIO UNIVERSITY
ATHENS, OHIO 45701

ORDER FROM:
Ohio University Press
Scott Quad, Ohio University
Athens, Ohio 45701

Out of Print volumes (marked with an *) can be obtained in microfilm or xerographic copies from University Microfilms International, at Box 1467, Ann Arbor, Michigan 48106 or 18 Bedford Row, London WCIR 4EJ, England.

Publication Number:

1 - TREASURES AND TRIVIA: Doctoral Dissertations on Southeast Asia Accepted by Universities in the United States. Compiled by Lian The and Paul W. van der Veur. 1968. 155 pp. $5.00
2 - PUBLIC PROTEST IN INDONESIA. By Ann Ruth Willner. 1968. 21 pp. $1.75
3*- DEVELOPMENTAL CHALLENGE IN MALAYSIA. By Siew Nim Chee. 1968.
4 - THE USE OF HISTORY. By Wang Gungwu. 1968. 24 pp. $1.75
5*- THE TRADITIONAL USE OF THE FORESTS IN MAINLAND SOUTHEAST ASIA. By James L. Cobban.
6*- CONFLICT AND POLITICAL DEVELOPMENT IN SOUTHEAST ASIA: An Exploration in the International Implications of Comparative Theory. By Gerald S. Maryanov.
7*- SRI PADUKA: The Exile of the Prince of Ayondha. Translated by S.M. Ponniah.
8 - AGRARIAN UNREST IN THE PHILIPPINES: Guardia de Honor--Revitalization within the Revolution; Rizalistas--Contemorary Revitalization Movements in the Philippines. By David R. Sturtevant. 1969. 1973 reprint. 44 pp. $2.75
9 - PANDANGGO-SA-ILAW: The Politics of Occidental Mindoro. By Remigio E. Agpalo. 1969. 32 pp. $2.00
10*- REPRESSION AND REVOLT: The Origins of the 1948 Communist Insurrection in Malaya and Singapore. By Michael R. Stenson.
11 - RUBBER AND THE MALAYSIAN ECONOMY: Implications of Declining Prices. By Tan Sri Lim Swee Aun. 1969. 36 pp. $2.50
12 - EDUCATION AND SOCIAL CHANGE IN COLONIAL INDONESIA: I. Progress and Procrastination in Education in Indonesia prior to World War II; II. The Social and Geographical Origins of Dutch-Educated Indonesians. By Paul W. van der Veur. 1969. 62 pp. $3.50
13*- COMMUNAL VIOLENCE IN MALAYSIA 1969: The Political Aftermath. By Felix V. Gagliano.
14*- SOVIET AND AMERICAN AID TO INDONESIA 1949-1968. By Usha Mahajani. 1970.
15*- POLITICS AMONG BURMANS: A Study of Intermediary Leaders. By John Badgley. 1970.
16 - TRADE AND EMPIRE IN MALAYA AND SINGAPORE, 1869-1874. By D. R. SarDesai. 1970. 22 pp. $1.75
17*- EXPANSION OF THE VIETNAM WAR INTO CAMBODIA: Action and Response by the Governments of North Vietnam, South Vietnam, Cambodia, and the United States. By Peter A. Poole. 1970.
18 - THE PRE-WORLD WAR II PERANAKAN CHINESE PRESS OF JAVA: A Preliminary Survey. By Leo Suryadinata. 1971. 44 pp. $2.75
19*- A REVIEW OF COMMUNITY-ORINETED ECOLOGICAL RESEARCH IN THE PHILIPPINES. By Robert A. Bullington. 1971.
20*- A BIBLIOGRAPHY OF PHILIPPINES LINGUISTICS. By Nobleza C. Asuncion-Landé. 1971.
21*- THE BURMA-YUNNAN RAILWAY: Anglo-French Rivalry in Mainland Southeast Asia and South China, 1895-1905. By J. Chandran.
22*- THE NORTH BORNEO CHARTERED COMPANY'S ADMINISTRATION OF THE BAJAU, 1878-1909: The Pacification of a Maritime, Nomadic People. By James F. Warren.
23*- PROMINENT INDONESIAN CHINESE IN THE TWENTIETH CENTURY: A Preliminary Survey. By Leo Suyandinata.
24 - PEACOCKS, PAGODAS, AND PROFESSOR HALL: A Critique of the Persisting Use of Historiography as an Apology for British Empire-Building in Burma. By Manuel Sarkisyanz. 1972. 68 pp. $3.50

25 - IMBALANCES IN DEVELOPMENT: The Indonesian Experience. By Selo Soemardjan. 1972. 26 pp. $2.00

26 - THE VERHANDELINGEN VAN HET BATAVIAASCH GENOOTSCHAP: An Annotated Content Analysis. Compiled by Lian The and Paul W. van der Veur. 1973. 150 pp. Index. $5.00

27 - JAPAN'S SCHEME FOR THE LIBERATION OF BURMA: The Role of the *Minami Kikan* and the "Thirty Comrades." By Won Z. Yoon. 1973. 65 pp. Bib. $3.50

28 - EDUCATIONAL SPONSORHIP BY ETHNICITY: A Preliminary Analysis of the West Malaysian Experience. By Yoshimitsu Takei, John C. Bock, and Bruce Saunders. 1973. 44 pp. $3.00

29 - BLOOD, BELIEVERS, AND BROTHER: The Development of Voluntary Associations in Malaysia. By Stephen A. Douglas and Paul Pederson. 1973. 119 pp. App. $4.50

30*- THE DYNAMICS OF POLITICS AND ADMINISTRATION IN RURAL THAILAND. By Clark D. Neher.

31 - PEASANT CITIZENS: Politics, Religion, and Modernization in Kelantan, Malaysia. By Manning Nash. 1974. 1977 reprint. 179 pp. Bib. $7.00

32 - MARGINAL MAN IN A COLONIAL SOCIETY: Abdoel Moeis' *Salah Asuhan*. By David de Queljoe. 1974. 43 pp. $3.00

33*- THE NEUTRALIZATION OF SOUTHEAST ASIA: An Analysis of the Malaysian/ASEAN Proposal. By Marvin C. Ott. 1974.

34 - THE LAND-TO-THE-TILLER PROGRAM AND RURAL RESOURCE MOBILIZATION IN THE MEKONG DELTA OF SOUTH VIETNAM. By C. Stuart Callison. 1974. 48 pp. $3.00

35 - THE FUTURE OF BURMA IN PERSPECTIVE: A Symposium. Edited and with an Introduction by Josef Silverstein. 1974. 104 pp. $4.50

36 - INDOCHINE: Perspectives for Reconciliation. Edited and with an Introduction by Peter A. Poole. 1975. 92 pp. $4.25

37 - THE COMINTERN AND VIETNAMESE COMMUNISM. By William J. Duiker. 1975. 48 pp. $3.25

38 - BROKER, MEDIATOR, PATRON AND KINSMAN: An Historical Analysis of Key Leadership Roles in a Rural Malaysian District. By Connor Bailey. 1976. 89 pp. Bib. LC 75-620141. $4.25

39 - CHIEF EXECUTIVES IN BLACK AFRICA AND SOUTHEAST ASIA: A Descriptive Analysis of Social Background and Characteristics. By Edward Baum and Felix Gagliano. 1976. 43 pp. App. $3.00

40 - FREEMASONRY IN INDONESIA FROM RADERMACHER TO SOEKANTO, 1762-1961. By Paul W. van der Veur. 1976. 42 pp. $3.25

41 - CULTURAL-ECOLOGICAL PERSPECTIVES ON SOUTHEAST ASIA: A Symposium. Edited and with an Introduction by William Wood. 1977. 192 pp. ISBN 0-8214-0322-2. LC 76-620062. $8.00

42 - SOUTHEAST ASIA, AN EMERGING CENTER OF WORLD INFLUENCE? ECONOMIC AND RESOURCE CONSIDERATIONS. Edited and introduced by Wayne Raymdond and K. Mulliner. Comments by Laurence D. Stifel. 1977. 136 pp. ISBN 0-8214-0324-9. LC 76-620090. $6.00

43 - POLLUTION AND POLITICS IN THE PHILIPPINES. By Ross Marlay. 1977. 131 pp. ISBN 0-8214-0325-7. LC 76-620091. $6.00

44 - INCOME, EMPLOYMENT, AND FOOD SYSTEMS IN JAVANESE COASTAL VILLAGES. By William L. Collier, Harjadi Hadikoesworo, and Suwardi Saropie. 1977. 160 pp. Maps, Tables, Glossary, Bib. ISBN 0-89680-031-8. LC 77-620017. $7.00

45 - FOREVER PLURAL: The Perception and Practice of Inter-Communal Marriage in Singapore. By Chew Sock Foon and John A. MacDougall. 1977. 67 pp. Tables, Bib. ISBN 0-89680-030-X. LC 77-620031. $3.75

46 - THAILAND, DOMINO BY DEFAULT? The 1976 Coup and Implications for United States Policy. With an Epilogue on the October 1977 Coup. By William Bradley, David Morell, David Szanton, and Stephen Young. 1978. 67 pp. ISBN 0-89680-032-6. LC 77-620050. $3.75

47 - COSMOLOGY AND SOCIAL BEHAVIOR IN A WEST JAVANESE SETTLEMENT. By Robert Wessing. Forthcoming 1978.

48 - SOUTHEAST ASIAN REFERENCES IN THE BRITISH PARLIAMENTARY PAPERS, 1801-1972/73: An Index. Compiled, Edited, and Introduced by Thomas F. Willer. 1978. 106 pp. ISBN 0-89680-033-4. LC 77-620064. $5.00

49 - AGRICULTURAL PRODUCTION AND HOUSEHOLD BUDGETS IN A SHAN PEASANT VILLAGE IN NORTHEASTERN THAILAND: A Quantitative Description. By E. Paul Durrenberger. 1978. 154 pp. Tables. ISBN 0-89680-071-7. $6.50

50 - Robustiano Echaúz' SKETCHES OF THE ISLAND OF NEGROS. Translated by Donn V. Hart with an Introduction by John A. Larkin. 1978. 174 pp. Glossary, Bib., Index. ISBN 0-89680-070-9. LC 78-13403. $7.00

51 - MAYORS AND MANAGERS IN THAILAND: The Struggle for Political Life in Administrative Settings. By Ronald L. Krannich. 1978. 139 pp. ISBN 0-89680-073-3. $6.00

ALSO: INTERNATIONAL BIOGRAPHICAL DIRECTORY OF SOUTHEAST ASIA SPECIALISTS. Compiled by Robert O. Tilman. 1969. 373 pp. Special price: $1.25

SEARCH FOR NEW GUINEA'S BOUNDARIES: From Torres Strait to the Pacific. By Paul W. van der Veur. ANU Press, 1966. 176 pp. $10.00